# THE PEOPLE'S BUS:

# STORIES FROM A LIFETIME

**JOHN CORREA**

1/21/17

Dear Jenny,

This really feels like a team effort with lots of help and lessons from the inside out!

Thanks so much for your encouragement and support.

Just asking for an occasional chuckle!

Love,
John

Best Wishes
John X. Correa
( official book
signing signature!)

ISBN: 1539807916

Copyright

ISBN-13: 978-1539807919

Cover: Lea Andersson

# Dedication:

*To the Master Teachers and Wayshowers*
*for their generous help, guidance, and inspiration.*

*The two offices of memory are collection and distribution.*

---Samuel Johnson

# Contents

# 1

# INTRODUCTION

*Your tale, sir, would cure deafness.*

---William Shakespeare, The Tempest

### The Storyteller

I grew up in a big family of seven kids.  Our dinners each night were loud, raucous rituals: politics were discussed, stories told, and future skills for finding a place in the world were forged in the crucible of the world's toughest audience i.e. my own brothers and sisters.  If I could win them over or hold them at bay, how difficult would workplace dynamics be years later?

I was making the transition from teacher to administrator in my elementary school years ago when a few old teacher friends thought it would be funny to heckle me from the back as I spoke to the staff for the first time as the Assistant Principal.  I cut them down to size as quickly and deftly as a stand-up comedian in a Las Vegas nightclub.  I then turned to the faculty and said, "I have been trained by the best teachers imaginable, my siblings, in how to hold the floor when speaking.  Please don't mess with me."  And they never did again.

Holding court at the dinner table was a difficult challenge.  This was a very tough crowd.  If you weren't funny, interesting, or able to captivate, they would tell you to shut up, ignore you, or talk over you.  If you were on your game, they were very responsive and would appreciate the humor if you could hold their attention long enough to get them through the necessary setups.

It was so loud that normal table manners, out of necessity, were ignored. "Pass the salt, will you" was lost in the din. Even calling someone out by name, "Drew, pass the salt" wasn't heard or was ignored. We just reached over the others when we needed something. On the rare occasion when our parents decided to take us out to dinner, we were like the *Lord Of The Flies* characters gone to finishing school. Suddenly we were placing napkins on our laps, switching hands with our forks, and talking at a civilized decibel count unlike dinners at home where the noise level was comparable to a Boeing 747 revving its engines.

We didn't know it back then, but were we taking an ongoing course in life training. When you grow up in a big family, you learn how to function in a group. You don't have to wait for school or a job to teach you that. You tend not to have an inflated sense of yourself. No one is hanging on your every word. "How was your day, Johnny?" Those were words I never heard, simply because no one cared and there was no time for that kind of indulgent questioning.

Because there are many rapid-fire conversations, comments, and asides, the dinner table is a great place to hone your wit. Humor in a big family is highly-valued and appreciated. You know you're reaching your audience when you can get the whole table laughing. Yet at the same time this is the toughest jury of your peers imaginable. Compliments are rare, and no one will acknowledge any skills, achievements, or honors. When I hit my one-and-only home run in Little League, the discussion at the dinner table that night was about my two strikeouts. Hard to become full of myself when I never head a compliment from a sibling.

To grow up being at ease with all this give-and-take translates into an ideal workplace skill. In addition, a light self-effacing sense of humor is generally very much appreciated at work. Where we can be a bit overwhelming to others is when we are faced with those who grew up in small families. They were accustomed to dinners growing up in which the family hung on their every word and everyone spoke in turn. It is our tendency to interrupt. In a big family we interrupt because we know where you're going and just cut you off at the pass to save time and keep the conversation moving forward. Out in the world we learn to rein in this tendency, especially when people become indignant because what they have to say is so important to them. "I'm not finished!" is what they will often say. That kind of a comment would be laughable at the chaotic big-family dinner table.

A really good story teller will not be denied. If interrupted, he will patiently wait. If off on a tangent, he will relentlessly, like a pitbull, wind his way back to the main narrative. He understands that hyperbole and embellishment are tools that if applied at precisely the right moment, can propel a story into pure magic. Yet there was always a price to be paid for this at our dinner table. The storyteller had, of course, stopped eating to tell his story. His audience had not. In a family in which a depression-era mother believed in just enough rather than more-than-enough, the storyteller paid. There were no leftovers. He would get less to eat than the others. The story had better be worth telling!

Once at my elementary school, a soon-to-be retired teacher, Colleen Cooke, went to the Social Security office during her prep period. She was mistreated by a mean, old woman and seemingly had a negative experience. But this wasn't how Colleen, a great storyteller, looked at it. Instead, she knew it would be funny in the retelling and couldn't wait for lunch time in the faculty room where she could regale her fellow teachers with her tale of woe and mimic the ornery employee. This is the essence of this kind of funny story: a person gets in trouble or has some unpleasant experience. Then, through self-effacing humor, a unique point of view, and a little embellishment, the audience can identify and laugh with the dilemma. Who can't relate to being mistreated by some government employee or salesperson?

My brother Bill has a gift for storytelling. Even as a young boy he was funny at the dinner table. He parlayed his speaking skills into a career of convincing people to join him in whatever project or endeavor in which he was involved.  He was always good at holding court and seemed to have a funny take on experiences he was having.  But it wasn't until he was in his fifties that he found himself in an experience that became the ultimate in 'Wow, this doesn't look good now, but it will be really, really funny in the retelling.'

A number of years ago, Bill took some family members to a Broadway show in New York City during the Christmas holidays. One of the great advantages of living in Hoboken, New Jersey just across the Hudson River from Manhattan is the quick access to the city and all it has to offer.  After a pleasant evening spent at the theatre seeing a play called *Bombay Dreams*, Bill retrieved the car from the parking lot and headed out with his family for the Lincoln Tunnel.  As they approached the tunnel, there were a number of police cars with their lights flashing, pulling cars over. Saturday night, leaving the city, must be a random sobriety check, Bill thought as he too was stopped.  It turned out he had a broken tail light.

"The officer took my license and registration.  When he returned, I expected him to give me a ticket or tell me to get it fixed as soon as possible.  No, instead, he told me to get out of the car.  He had me spread-eagle against the police car and summarily announced that I was under arrest.  There was an outstanding warrant for a speeding ticket from twenty-three years earlier when I was visiting the Hamptons out on Long Island.

"The next thing I know I was handcuffed and led away to a police prison bus parked on the shoulder.  I could hear my family still pleading with the officers as I was hustled onto the bus, but at least they didn't impound the car and allowed my wife to drive it back to Hoboken, broken tail light and all.

"When I entered the bus, I counted nine people aboard.  All were handcuffed to their seats as would be my fate, too.  There we were, all white out-of-towners apparently being scammed in a police revenue-raising bust.

"Off we rode to the Midtown precinct. I was put into a jail cell with another guy waiting to get booked.  After fingerprinting and the mug shot, I was returned to the cell, which was now starting to fill up with real criminals:  muggers, drug dealers, and other violent offenders.  A guy was brought in wearing drab gray police pajamas.  His blood-stained clothes had been confiscated for evidence.  He claimed that someone was thrown down the stairs toward him on a crowded staircase at a nightclub and fell onto the knife he was carrying in his pocket.  There were now eleven guys jammed into the cell, and all proclaimed their innocence.

"I had called my wife Karin a couple of times, telling her that I expected to be released at any moment.  But it was about 1:00 AM when a cop announced to us that we would be going to central booking at the notorious Tombs Prison.  Back on the bus, we went around to various precincts to collect the accused.  By the time we reached the Tombs, there were thirty-five of us on aboard, all, you guessed it, cuffed to our seats.  This was not a crowd of loiterers or toll jumpers.  They talked like they knew the routine.

"Once at the Tombs I still thought I would be getting out at any moment.  I asked the admitting cop how I could possibly get a driver's license with an outstanding ticket?  I've had a number of licenses over these twenty-three years.  He just assumed I had fake ones.

"The Tombs was scary.  Seven levels down, all steel.  It was gruesome, like something out of the movies.   A part of me was like a tourist:  wow, interesting, cool!  I was headed down into the bowels of criminal justice!  But I'd be out of here any moment.   It's already way past my bed time!

"We were taken down six levels. This floor was all cells.  I was put in a big cell with twenty other alleged perpetrators.  I was the only white person.  All the other guys were black and Hispanic and looked like this wasn't their first visit.  There I was dressed in a blue cashmere sweater, Brooks Brothers corduroys, and tasseled Italian loafers.  I was reminded of the scene in the 1980 movie *Stir Crazy* in which Richard Pryor and Gene Wilder were about to enter a huge cell packed with hardened criminals. Richard Pryor starts strutting and bobbing up and down.

'What are you doing?' asks the Gene Wilder character.

'I'm getting bad,' responds Pryor, 'so they don't mess with us.'

As they enter the cell Gene Wilder is bobbing and gyrating just like Richard Pryor. 'That's right, we're bad. We don't take no shit,' they say in unison.

"The other prisoners just stared at them unamused, and annoyed that they were making such a unwanted commotion.

"But what was I worrying about? I'd be out of here momentarily once someone realized I was in the wrong place.

"Then we got the news that the night judge had gone home. It was now 2:00 AM on December 31$^{st}$.   My cellmates were just thinking about survival.  Most had been arrested multiple times.  Some just lay down and went to sleep on the concrete floor.   It's funny:  even though some were facing five years in prison, their main concern was the strong possibility that they would be missing  the upcoming New Year's Eve parties.

"One guy told the story of how he was arrested for dealing cocaine. He didn't seem concerned about the repercussions.  He remained fixated on his anger with his partner who escaped by jumping out a window, leaving him to get caught on the roof.

"Another fellow detainee was tackled by the police causing his shoes to get scuffed.  He couldn't stop talking about this apparent indignity as if the condition of his shoes mattered more in the scheme of things than what he was facing.   Evidently he was perturbed that a status symbol in his world had been violated.

"There was a phone in the cell.   We could call collect, but the phone company charged two dollars a minute.  The families wouldn't accept the calls once they saw it was from the Tombs.  They had been burned before and weren't going to get stuck with a fifty-dollar phone bill they couldn't afford.

"I got through the night by becoming a jailhouse lawyer for the other guys.  Some of them were illiterate so I would read the charges out loud for them.  The captive audience would laugh in recognition when they heard the allegations and were able to quickly rattle off the mandatory minimum sentencing:  "Assault. You're fucked.  That's three to five years."

"I was also busy handing out quarters, which for some reason I seemed to have a supply of, for phone calls.  Eventually someone asked me, 'What are you in for?'  A speeding ticket from twenty-three years ago.  Everyone laughed. 'The "Man" is after you!'  Now that I had criminal cred, my cellmates and I bonded like long-lost fellow gang members.

"At about 6:00 AM, 'breakfast' arrived:  baloney sandwiches on Wonder Bread.  I hadn't eaten one of those since childhood.  My Trader Joe's foodie sensibility made the idea of eating it unthinkable.  I just gave it away.  There was something about the Tombs that took away my appetite, nor did I want to scrape this food imposter off the roof of my mouth.

"At nine in the morning, the judges returned and the review of the cases began.  The police officers would come down to the cells to escort us to the courtrooms.  'I need ten more pieces' I heard one cop yell.  It turned out he was referring to us, the detainees, in jail jargon. We were 'pieces of shit.'

"By six o'clock that evening, I still hadn't been called.  Finally I met with a Legal Aid lawyer.  She advised me to plead guilty so they would let me out.

"I was put into another holding tank where a fight almost broke out. Another detainee told me he was arrested for selling batteries on Madison Avenue.  Because he had been arrested numerous times for this so-called crime, it was likely he would end up on Riker's Island, the long-term version of the Tombs.

"As as it got later and later, I had to sweat out the possibility that the judges would leave early since it was now New Year's Eve. Finally, I appeared before the judge and pled guilty.  I had thirty days to pay the hundred dollar fine.

"Days later, I went to the Hamptons to clear up the mess.  They told me that there had been a computer glitch and even though the records showed I had paid the ticket, I would have to pay it again to expunge it from the system.  So I had to pay $230 to clear it, plus $100 to the court in New York City, plus $80 in collect calls from the Tombs that my wife thankfully accepted after I ran out of quarters.

"In our last phone conversation, I told Karin as I did in all the previous calls that I was just about to be released.  I was confident enough to tell her that I would meet her at the party we had been invited to.  I finally arrived close to midnight. I asked for a drink.  And then I had a story to tell."

Beyond Bill's adaptable behavior and his ability to relate humorously "a man in trouble story," I was taken by the Kafkaesque nature of his ordeal.  He was living the nightmare of a bizarre and impersonal administrative situation in which he felt powerless to understand or control what was happening.  Could the Tombs have been even more of a living hell than a setting taken directly from one of Kafka's novels?

*The Trial* is the story of a man arrested and prosecuted by a remote, inaccessible authority,  the nature of his crime never revealed to him. Likewise, Bill was temporarily caught between the faceless bureaucracies of two governmental systems: New York State and New York City.  The ending was a relatively happy one even though it cost Bill some extra money. He was eventually awakened from his nightmare, avoiding a transfer, fortunately, to the dreaded Riker's Island Prison.

I love that Bill was able to apply his big family skills to a challenging situation.  He found a way to fit into a group with which he had precious little in common.  He was quick on his feet and used his communications skills to become useful to the other detainees.  He not only survived, but thrived, winning acceptance for outrunning "The Man" for twenty-three years.  Best of all, Bill helped out some of the guys by feeding them quarters and reading the criminal charges to the illiterate.  He found a way to adapt just as he did growing up in a big family.  Bill never thought he would face a more difficult audience than his siblings until he was locked up in a jail cell at the Tombs.  In the end he was able to rely on his invaluable training from his childhood.  This anecdote, re-told many times, was not only a bonus to a trying circumstance, but a signature story that has gone down in family lore as the gold standard.   Who among us will ever top it?

# 2

# TRAVEL

*The traveler sees what he sees.*
*The tourist sees what he has come to see.*

**---G.K. Chesterton**

### The People's Bus

In the fall of 1974, my brother Dick and I were enjoying some post graduation travel south of the border. In Mexico City, we visited the shrine of the Virgin of Guadalupe, the patron saint of Mexico revered throughout the Americas. Part of her appeal is that her alleged appearance to an indigenous man, Juan Diego, helped to convert the native people of Mexico to Christianity. As we sat in the shade wolfing down the delicious tamales we bought from a street vendor, we noticed the long procession of tour buses arriving with military precision. Even with a pilgrimage as sacred as this is to devout Catholics, the mode of transportation for many was the tour bus. This same scene no doubt plays out at more secular destinations like Fisherman's Wharf, the Eiffel Tower, and just about any other tourist site on the must see checklist.

I've often wondered why visitors to foreign countries so willingly give up their individuality and allow themselves to be shepherded around like members of a quarantined chain gang. Not willing to leave their comfort zones? Afraid for their safety? Perhaps a belief that the natives are out to get 'em? Worried that in the local market haggling for a tourist trinket, they may get fleeced? A bilingual tour guide will be just the buffer to all this potential unpleasantness and the anxiety that often accompanies the unknown.  Pity these poor people in the tour buses doomed to their canned experiences and denied  interactions with the local people. Separating oneself from the host culture is not a prescription for adventure.   Riding public transportation, on the other hand, increases the likelihood of some interesting encounters.

We continued our travels by regular bus, making our way through southern Mexico. We crossed into Guatemala at the border town of Mesilla, arriving at our first bus station in the western highlands.  We immediately recognized some old friends.  Our ancient, beat up, yellow school buses from grade school that we thought were sold for scrap metal or occasionally converted into  "hippie mobiles" when it was time for them to be taken off the road were actually  sold to bus companies in Latin America.  These junkers undergo a stunning metamorphosis as they are magically transformed and restored.  Rebuilt engines are installed, and bright paint is carefully applied in elaborate and pleasing-to-the-eye combinations.  Racks are installed on top for the various wares and items riders bring to the market to sell or for purchases to take home.

The conductor, usually a tireless teenager, collects fares and scurries up and down the outside ladder moving bundles and bags (and occasional chickens) with lightning speed, trying to help the driver stay on schedule despite numerous stops.

We caught one of these classic "chicken buses" bound for the famous Mayan market town, Chichicastenango.   Little did we know that one of the quintessential Guatemalan experiences, riding a "camioneta," was about to become ours.

As we boarded, our attention was immediately riveted beneath the dashboard to an elaborate shrine dedicated to a familiar face, the Virgin of Guadalupe.  It consisted of a prominently displayed statue surrounded by plastic flowers and a dangling row of blinking Christmas lights.  All was very quaint and colorful until we experienced a few speedy hairpin turns on the treacherous mountain roads followed by terrifying vistas of precipitous drops to canyons below. If that weren't enough, being subjected to the unnerving aggression of a lead-footed driver made us quickly realize that the shrine might well be our life-line. As one precarious curve after another presented itself, even the most cynical, and at this point white-knuckled atheist, slowly but surely would turn a petitioning eye toward what had now become a personal savior bobbling along in the shrine up front. If there were room in the aisle, it now would seem totally appropriate to prostrate oneself at the feet of our "Lady" in fervent and devout prayer...

We had no idea about the scenery we were about to encounter. If ever there were a true "God's country," it is this region of Guatemala. The Cuchumatanes Mountains are a dazzling display of forested ridges thick with pine, cedar, and oak amidst gushing streams above plunging verdant valleys containing patchwork fields of maize and potatoes. Heading south we were transfixed by the majestic volcanoes, and because a plateau runs right through the middle of the country, the altitude allows for pine trees to grow alongside palm trees. It has one of the world's most delightful climates with "eterna primavera" (eternal spring), as it is often described.

Off we went enjoying the friendliness and hospitality of our fellow riders as we had the opportunity to practice our basic Spanish. Of course it is the language of food, lodging, and travel that are first to show vast improvement as they are born of necessity. We were also glad to have our attention taken off the hair-raising drive and all the "is it my time to buy the farm" scenarios.

It was no surprise then as the trip lengthened and the bus bumped and lurched along that our discomfort grew. The spacious leg room we enjoyed many years before as elementary school kids had shrunk, of course, now that we were adults. Since our knees were jammed up against the seats in front of us, we pretty much needed a crowbar to extricate ourselves.  Our fellow travelers chuckled heartily when a tall blond gringo from central casting for "California surfer" untangled his long legs, stood up, and began vigorously massaging his cramping hamstrings. It was easy to read the silent words hanging in the air:  "Mala suerte, gringo.  You see, there are advantages to being five foot four."

I hadn't been feeling particularly well at the onset of our trip, and my condition suddenly worsened as a wave of nausea overcame me.  I announced to the passenger sitting next to me, "Estoy enfermo." He offered to switch places so I could be next to the window in the hope that the fresh air would settle down my queasy stomach.  I've always loved that the word for tourists and the traveling sickness they get is the same in Spanish: "turista."   By the time we pulled into a gas station in a remote pueblo, I felt so sick I didn't know if I could make it to the grungy bathroom, nor did I know from which end of my body a huge explosion was about to issue forth.  Trudging unsteadily, I made it to the baño but was dismayed to discover a toilet with no seat and a pile of ripped up newspaper for toilet paper.  We're told that women will hover when they don't like the looks of a toilet seat and that the true germaphobes hover over all public toilets.  Well, I had neither the skill nor energy in my weakened condition to even attempt it.  I just plopped down unceremoniously on the rim.  There I waited for whatever was going to happen, just sitting there for a few minutes when suddenly I was startled by someone kicking open the door and shouting "Vamanos."  It was the driver, irate that he was falling behind his sacrosanct schedule.

I did my best to pull myself together, but by the time I made it back outside, there was no sign of the bus.  "Jesus Christ," I wailed out loud, "my brother has now abandoned me at some isolated cantina in the hinterlands of Guatemala."  Almost worse, I had the irritating realization that I probably would have been better off booking one of those goddamn tour buses I had so contemptuously belittled.

Meanwhile, back in the bus, a number of passengers were speaking up on behalf of my brother urging the driver to wait, telling him he couldn't leave this guy's brother behind. The driver said he was already behind schedule and couldn't wait any longer.

I looked to my left and there was the bus about two hundred yards down the road chugging along fitfully in first gear as the driver evidently was still arguing with his passengers. Because my survival was at stake, I somehow was able to find a strength I didn't know I possessed and began to run toward the bus as some divinely-graced adrenaline, perhaps even some good vibes resulting from my newly found adoration for my patron saint, the Virgin of Guadalupe, kicked in. As I approached the moving bus, the former emergency exit, now the back door, miraculously opened up. Before I knew what was happening, many extended hands reached out and lifted me up and into the bus. I must have had the most astonished look on my face as I suddenly landed in the aisle as if transported through some invisible realm. There was pandemonium as the passengers exploded into full out belly-laugh mode. My brother Dick, by now an honorary Guatemalteco, joined in the merriment. Yet I didn't feel as if anyone was laughing at me. On the contrary, the passengers were with me one hundred percent as I felt their brotherhood, humanity, and empathy envelop me. I so appreciated their intuitive understanding that family, and one brother looking out for another, is a cause that they, these good people of Guatemala, could get behind.

Again, I was placed gingerly next to a window. The estudiante de medicina on board checked me out, but I was on the road to recovery energized by the wave of concern and sympathy shown by these beautiful people. Each and every passenger before disembarking came back to my seat to wish me well and say goodbye. I felt like an honored guest, grateful for the common humanity shared between the two cultures.

# Saddle Up

I had always wanted to travel to Europe.  Student loans and work had derailed my plans for doing the Eurorail backpacking ritual like many of my friends did when they were younger.  In my early thirties, I decided to quit my dead-end job as an adjunct instructor of remedial English at my local community college and head off for Europe.

I spent the summer of 1985 traversing Scandinavia before heading south into Italy and  the Greek Isles.  On Crete, I decided to extend my trip and set sail for the Middle East where I could fulfill a life-long dream to visit Egypt and experience the fabled pyramids.

I was always fascinated by the significance of the pyramids in the occult world and captivated by what I had read.  Having studied the geometric astral energy points and having pondered the "Eye of Providence" peering out from the top of the Cheops, the grandest of all pyramids, I was pinching myself that I would get to see one of the "Seven Wonders of the World" up close.

"And how is it that the single eye and the pyramid appear on the back of the one-dollar bill?"  I would ask friends back home whenever the topic came up, feeling a sense of  astonishment and deep-seated curiosity.

So, I fully expected that something significant would transpire in Egypt.  It was just too much of a setup and surely not a coincidence that events had conspired to bring me to this mysterious land of esoteric secrets.

My first night in Egypt, my fellow traveling companions and I made our way to Giza to attend the light and sound show at the great pyramids. I was captivated as the narrator at one point intoned "The world fears time.  Time fears the pyramids."

"Never heard anything more touristy or hokey," commented Larry Wilson, a fellow traveler who really knew how to put a damper on the enthusiasm of others, however innocent or naïve it may have been. Still these unique structures thrilled me as did their grandeur and sheer scale.

"Wow, Cheops is as tall as a 48-story building and for forty-three centuries was the tallest man-made structure on earth until the Eiffel Tower was built in the 1800's," I marveled out loud to my nearby audience of fellow tourists, careful to be out of Larry's earshot.

We discovered that it was possible to take a camel ride from the great pyramid of Cheops to the site of the original step pyramids some eighteen miles away in Saqqara. After a unanimous vote, our intrepid party of willing adventurers decided to return the next morning, looking forward to what we thought would be an engrossing history lesson as well as a chance to travel like the Egyptians of antiquity through the windswept dunes of the iconic Sahara Desert. And as for me, I was anticipating that something unexpected would be revealed at the original site of these ancient temples. Why I thought this and what it would be, I had no idea, just an intuitive feeling that some major insight or life-changing understanding was coming my way.

When we arrived the next morning at the pyramids, the scene was one of swirling chaos identical to what Mark Twain had described a century earlier in *Innocents Abroad*. We were accosted by hordes of young people angling and jostling for position to perform any possible service in hopes of receiving the precious "baksheesh." One of the first words that tourists learn in Arabic, it can mean alms, tip, or bribe. No matter where tourists go in Egypt, some indigent beggar or street kid will ask for baksheesh. Sometimes it is rudely demanded but ever so graciously accepted by the natives in return often for little or no services rendered.

I have to admit that before we arrived at the Pyramids, I had experienced a typical Egyptian baksheesh scam. An uninvited tour guide began to lead a few of us on a tour of Cairo without any initial talk of compensation.  I let it go on too long, thinking that maybe this was the interaction that was going to lead to whatever situation or person I was supposed to meet. It was difficult not only because I didn't know what I was looking for, but there were no signs I could see or interpret.  I was left trying to trust my intuition since there was nothing concrete to light the way.  This particular situation ended badly with exorbitant baksheesh demands by my unsolicited "tour guide."

Another time, I was hounded by a couple of insistent scammers trying to sell "the world's best perfume."  Out to a desert oasis I trooped, only to be told that the sweet smelling flowers growing there were the essential ingredients of the great perfumes of Paris.  I suspected that was just a cover and that I had truly arrived at  a secret site at which some esoteric unveiling of the key to understanding ancient hieroglyphics would be revealed to me. Eventually recognizing that no, this really was about perfume, and feeling gullible, I succumbed to the aggressive sales pitch and bought a couple of small bottles for my mother just to get these crazy con-men out of my hair.  I still enjoyed the experience, however, as I knew the possibility always existed that one thing could lead to another, particularly in a situation in which a revelation seemed unlikely to occur.

Larry, on the other hand, avoided these kinds of interactions at all costs.  It was as if every Egyptian that approached him had leprosy.

"You can't trust these people.  They're all out to get our money," he said derisively.

At Cheops that morning, after hearing that a long camel ride would be torture on the back,  our traveling group decided it would be best to rent horses.  There was no overruling this decision.  I couldn't very well admit my little secret that I had a life-long fear of horses and had never ridden one.  It would have been out of place to impose my view that we should reconsider riding the camels since everyone else wanted to avoid the back discomfort that we had been warned about.  In addition, I did not relish the emasculating idea of sheepishly slinking back to the hotel and missing this once-in-a-lifetime opportunity to visit the step pyramids, nor the inevitable ridicule that Larry would certainly supply.

To avoid any such mockery, I decided to reach out to Larry and tell him the truth about my phobia, hoping he would understand my dilemma and be sympathetic. We had a few minutes alone, so I just launched in on a story I felt compelled to tell.

"I have always been afraid of horses, Larry. Just like dogs, they can sense fear. And knowing that they know has only made me more afraid. Growing up in an area of New Jersey that hadn't quite transformed from exurban to suburban, there were still plenty of horses around. I can remember as clear as day that finicky old stallion, Sugar, who occasionally grazed in a lush pasture next to our house. My brothers and sisters loved to feed it ripe crab apples from a nearby tree and affectionately stroke its mane. I was wary of those big teeth and protruding gums that would make a periodontist salivate. My concern was losing a finger or getting too close and risking a kick to the head.

"Then one day when I was nine-years-old my worst fears were realized. Sugar was out grazing in the middle of the pasture when he suddenly galloped over to where my brother Billy and I were standing just inside the gate. There was no time to climb over the fence as Sugar became agitated and reared up, neighing frantically. I was terrified as I felt two quick kicks, one to the solar plexus and the other square on the chin, that left me crumpled in acute pain. I couldn't breathe, and I could feel the blood streaming down my chin. Billy yelled for our older brothers, and I ended up in the emergency room with ten stitches and a scar that to this day looks like I was in an old style gang knife fight."

"You wimp. You're like someone who nearly drowned and avoided the water and swimming lessons for the rest of your life," Larry said scornfully. "Now you're screwed. Good luck learning on the fly."

So much for empathy.   True, I had done my best to avoid horses and never mounted or rode one. It didn't matter that I was wiry and athletic. I was still traumatized:   no pony rides, no dude ranches, no wilderness excursions with pack horses.  I always kept my distance.  I didn't let myself get talked into getting on some frisky horse that would take off at a gallop, and then when the mood struck throw me unceremoniously to the ground.

I was now stuck in a situation in which I had no other option.   And this wasn't going to be some ring-around-the-rosy ride on a Shetland pony.  No, I was facing a good thirty-five mile roundtrip that would take at least nine hours to complete.   It would be baptism under fire!

At the stable, Larry acted as the lead negotiator and haggled so persistently that the Egyptian stable owner threw up his hands and agreed to the rock bottom price just to finally silence this "Ugly American."

Ahmad, an Egyptian teenager riding on a donkey, was assigned to be the guide.  One look at the horse pen would have been enough for any S.P.C.A. member to howl in protest.  The horses were malnourished, their living conditions were dreadful, and the whippings constant.  In a third-world country, animals are viewed much differently.  If any of us were to tell an Egyptian that his donkey had "animal rights," he would collapse in convulsions of laughter.  Many are still beasts of burden; they surely aren't viewed as pets.  We cringed when we witnessed the whippings and rough treatment the stable hands and owners meted out, and we  knew our guide would be using that long, thin stick he was holding to prod and beat the horses on our trip into the Sahara.

Ahmad gave me a boost to help me mount my horse.  There were no instructions for the novice.  Immediately, I had my hands full as I hung on for dear life.  It was one of those learn-by-doing situations, so I grabbed the reins and tried to imitate the technique of the more experienced riders.  As we set off and passed in front of the Cheops Pyramid, I was unsteady, unsure of myself, and trying to adjust to Abdul, the poor wretch of a horse assigned to me.  This sorry excuse for a horse was missing its two front teeth.  I had never seen that before.  He was gray with a white marking on his face and noticeably smaller than the other horses.  Scrawny and mangy, Abdul lacked regular grooming and could have used a makeover.  What stood out most was his passive-aggressive, docile-defiant behavior, demonstrated by his annoying habit of taking a few quick steps and then immediately slowing down.  This was wreaking havoc on my lower back and made me think that the camels would have been a much more comfortable option after all.

In November, the desert heat in the Sahara is tolerable.  Temperatures are in the eighties, but the sun is still penetrating enough for foreign travelers to dress like wanna-be Bedouins with colorful Egyptian scarves covering their heads and flowing long sleeve shirts to prevent sunburn.  Unlike the Bedouins, however, we strangers from distant continents had a virtually constant desert thirst that necessitated carrying plenty of water in our packs.

As the caravan began making its way from Giza out into the desert, we suddenly heard a commotion from the dune above us.  We watched with astonishment as if a scene from the movie *Lawrence of Arabia* was playing out in front of us.  In the film, the Omar Sharif character was first seen as just a dot on the horizon.  He then rode at full gallop right to where a delirious Lawrence was waiting.  In virtually a cinematic replay, an Arab dressed in full black desert regalia just like Omar, charged down the dune right towards us and then galloped off, disappearing over the next dune as if on some emergency mission.  The disturbance spooked Larry's horse causing it to rear up, almost throwing helpless Larry to the ground.

I laughed happily at my know-it-all tourist acquaintance getting a bit of comeuppance.

"You know Larry, you really need to work on controlling your horse better. "

Once the words were out of my mouth, I regretted saying them as I felt a foreboding sense that they would come back to haunt me.

Part of the journey to the step pyramids at Saqqara involved leaving the desert for a small stretch and riding through a tiny village. Because we were on horses, the people didn't notice that we were Western tourists right away and went about their business as usual. I was shocked at the level of abject poverty. Garbage and old tires were strewn about in a putrid open sewer. The buildings were rundown stone hovels, many with windows missing and corrugated flat roofs held in place with bricks. The pace of life was beyond slow. The only activity was a group of little kids playing with an old wheel, rolling it along for entertainment. The few residents seemed listless. There was no sign of anyone working. We passed a man sitting by the side of a deeply rutted dirt pathway that was also the main road through town. He was missing an eye. Flies were congregating in his empty eye socket. He made no effort to swat them away. I paused for a few moments in front of this semi-blind pauper wondering if he were a Tiresias figure, the mystic seer, who would give me some sort of sign...

There were also one-legged beggars and mentally-ill people talking to themselves under the shade of a lemon tree. Even Larry was a bit shaken by what he saw and lapsed into silence.

My back was about to go into spasm as the convoy of horses and riders approached Saqqara. I was still at war with Abdul as his maddening three-step-trot followed by the immediate slowdown continued.

"Damn it, Abdul, can't you walk like a normal horse?" I pleaded to my stubborn  contrarian.

The guide continued his historical monologue as his captive audience learned that the step pyramids were built in 2,700 B.C. and were the precursors to the Giza pyramids which were built about 150 years later. When our group got their first good look at the sixteen pyramids spread out over a large area, we could see the effect of the erosion that occurred over the last 5,000 years. The pyramids are slowly disintegrating into the desert much like melting icebergs being reclaimed by the ocean.

Each step pyramid was designed to be a staircase to heaven. This wasn't a symbolic rendering of a ladder but, in Egyptian religious beliefs, an actual one by which the soul of the dead ruler might climb to the sky, joining the gods in immortality.

Damn, even these symbols of the great beyond aren't doing a thing for me, I thought to myself impatiently. Where is that elevating sense of oneness I was convinced I would experience out here?

The mastermind behind the design and construction of these extraordinary edifices was the uniquely-accomplished Imhotep. As the guide droned on we had become fatigued tourists struggling to stay attentive. The exception, as always, was Larry who continued with his incessant three-part questions.

Mr. Imhotep's achievements were drummed into us at every turn. We learned that he was the designer and chief architect of Djoser, the first and largest of the step pyramids. He was also a high priest, magician, writer, founder of Egyptian astronomy and architecture, chief physician, and chief of sculptors. After his death, he was elevated to the position of full deity.

As the afternoon sun was beginning to descend, I was getting a bit antsy and had heard enough about this too-good-to-be-true genius, Imhotep . He may have dwarfed the accomplishments of the West's revered Renaissance man, Leonardo Di Vinci, as the guide proudly pointed out, implying that Leonardo was a hopeless slacker by comparison, but I couldn't have cared less as my attention was riveted like the quintessential survivor, Odysseus, on the return trip home.

The question was whether I could survive another four-to-five-hour-ride on this reluctant and uncooperative beast back to the stable at Giza. It had now come down to a war-of-wills between Abdul and his rank beginner. I had tried everything: gentle on the reins, hard on the reins, soothing encouragement, patting his side. Nothing worked. Abdul refused to move in any way resembling a rhythmic gait. He would giddy up and then slow to a crawl, continuing to stress my lower back.

Abdul did not begin to pick up the pace like the other horses did as they sensed the turn for home and began to taste the end of the journey.

"What's the matter John, can't get your slow poke moving?"

"No, it's just Abdul listening to his different drummer."

God was this Larry guy annoying, but I couldn't blame Abdul in that regard. What was so appealing about returning to his rundown stable other than he didn't have to trot around or carry someone? I wondered.

So there we were, my horse and I meandering along when Abdul suddenly lowered his head. No one ever told me that was the one thing you just can't let a horse do. You must pull up on the reins to raise the head. Well, Abdul evidently was delighted with his rider's ignorance and just keeled over. I barely got one leg out of the stirrup as Abdul landed on top of my other leg. The other riders really thought this was hilarious, especially Larry who almost fell off his horse, this time because he was laughing so hard.

"He must be tired," Ahmad noted.

No kidding, I thought, after the way he's been beaten, malnourished, and overworked.

I dusted myself off while flashing on some of the greatest man and horse tandems: The Lone Ranger had Silver, Roy Rogers had Trigger, and Wilbur Post had Mr. Ed.  Well, like it or not, I had Abdul.

"Goddammit!" I screamed for all to hear.  "I am going to ride this fucking horse!"

I felt a sudden desire to take this "bull" by the horns.  I had enough.  Something clicked in my brain.  The dial moved from passive to aggressive.

*I am to be the master now, and you, Abdul, will serve me.*

Even Larry was quietly transfixed by this dramatic turn of events.  I would no longer be intimidated, nor willingly be a victim of Abdul's quirky behavior.

Once Ahmad got the horse back on its feet, I mounted him with a new resolve.  I yanked hard on the reins, pressed in hard with my thighs and took command.  Amazingly, my former contrarian responded.  Now instead of loping along, Abdul began to move like a horse.  He picked up speed, and before I knew it, we were in a full-out gallop.

"Wow, what a rush!"  I gleefully yelled at the top of my lungs.

It was absolutely thrilling to race up and down the steep dunes at breakneck speed, my  faithful companion, Abdul, leading the charge. My traveling acquaintances were left with the fading sound of my whoops and hollers  as the late afternoon autumn light had transformed the ordinary yellow sand into a dazzling and magical golden hue.

Now at long last, I understood why people love to ride horses!  And more importantly, I realized that my purpose for coming to Egypt had been sitting right under me all that time.

I woke up the next morning at the hotel, my buttocks and thigh muscles so sore that walking was a painfully slow one-step-at-a-time ordeal.  Nothing, however, could diminish my sense of accomplishment and satisfaction:  I had seen the pyramids, made peace with Abdul, and gotten to experience what riding a horse was really all about.  And although overcoming my fear of horses wasn't quite the mystic revelation I was hoping for, it felt like I got the experience I needed.  And you know, I've never felt the urge to ride a horse ever again...

# 3

# FAMILY

*The only people who truly know your story,*
*are the ones who help you write it.*

---Anonymous

## Oh Rats!

My father held the meat cleaver glistening in the bright winter sunshine, poised to strike as my brother Drew held the bag, ready to release the poisoned and listless rat. I was inside in the living room anxiously watching this scene unfold outside while I nervously gnawed on the seat cover of an upholstered armchair. My dad suddenly slashed downward with the cleaver, decapitating the rat and sending crimson red blood spurting onto the blinding, bleach-white snow.

This was the conclusive end to a mystery that had been plaguing our household for a number of days when I was growing up in the 1960's in suburban Monmouth County, New Jersey. It began when we would come down to breakfast each morning. We were baffled to discover that the bananas that we stored in a little basket on the kitchen table had big scoops taken out of them clear through the peels. My six siblings and I were mystified and theorized that maybe a chipmunk was responsible. This scenario repeated itself for a few consecutive mornings. We convinced our parents to keep putting the bananas out so we could see if the behavior continued. It did, as more scoops appeared each morning.

Then late one night, my father was reading quietly by himself in the library when a rat crept out from under the radiator. Dad didn't move a muscle as he observed the rodent hovering near the heater.

Following a brief consultation at the hardware store, Dad chose a poison that would cause the rat to die of thirst. He thought this approach would make it less likely the rat would die within the walls and create a repulsive stench. He placed the poison under the radiator, and we all waited for the next turn of events. The bananas went untouched, not that any of us could imagine slicing them up and adding them to our corn flakes anytime soon.

One morning a day or two later, Mom went into the laundry room screamed, and immediately ran out, slamming the door shut behind her. The rat, having ingested the poison, was hovering near the washing machine in search of water. My oldest brother, Drew, had the unenviable job of scooping the rat into a bag and then taking it outside for its impending execution.

As a little first grader I watched the beheading of the rat from the living room window. Afterwards, I couldn't get the image of the rat's dark red blood splattering onto the pure white snow out of my brain. That night, I went to bed primed to have a nightmare. Adding to my anxiety was the fact that my bedroom was right at the top of the stairs. I feared that it would be a likely first choice for a faceless fellow member of the pack intent on revenge, or in the mood to explore the upstairs spoils of bedroom snacking. In addition, the weathered dwelling we lived in had plenty of creaks, clanking steam radiators that whistled like rumbling freight trains, and unexplained noises and squeaks that sounded like hordes of unknown creatures up to no good. "This old house" was the ideal setting for fertile imaginations like mine.

Somehow, after lying there in wide-awake anxiety, I eventually fell asleep. Inevitably, a nightmare ensued. I dreamt there was a rat at the bottom of my bed gnawing at my feet. I woke up terrified and quickly jumped out of bed immediately lunging toward the doorway frantic to escape my nocturnal demon. My parents heard a blood-curdling shriek and raced to my room. They found me sprawled on the floor, motionless, a huge egg-like welt on my forehead.  The next day we had to piece together the sequence of events like police detectives since neither of my parents initially had any idea what had happened and the eye witness was found unconscious.  The only conclusion we could make from the circumstantial evidence was that I hit my head on the edge of the half-opened door in my panicked rush to escape the terror I believed the rodent was inflicting upon me.

Over the years, the rat dream became less frequent, but just when I thought it was gone forever, it would reappear like Halley's Comet but on shorter and more pronounced intervals.  Eventually, in my twenties, I decided to seek help.  There must have been some rat symbolism that I was missing.  I hoped that my therapist, Doctor Helga, who came highly recommended for making progress with the most difficult patients, would help me to make sense of this and find the understanding I was lacking.

Clinical Helga didn't pull any punches.  Since the rat was gnawing on my feet in the dream, she relentlessly explored that theme.   "Rats point to the threatening things going on inside of you that you're not clear about.  I specifically mean the underhanded side of yourself, the shadow and it's dirt and squalor.   I suspect these unacceptable parts of your psyche are slowly gnawing away at your life," she intoned confidently with seeming expertise.

"Yikes, Helga.  It's that bad?"   I asked despondently.

"And furthermore, the rat signifies feelings of doubt, greed, guilt, unworthiness, envy, repulsion, decay, and even death.  You are keeping something to yourself that is eating you up inside, or you have done something  you are not proud of."

"For God's sake, Doctor, I was six years old when I had this dream.  Wasn't it precipitated by a traumatic event?"  I asked a bit bewildered.

"The good news for you, John, is that the gnawing could represent your inquisitive, searching side as you seek out meaning and answers in your life. More likely, the gnawing relates to your anxieties, self-questioning, and your worrying mind that disturbs or eats away at things like peace of mind or self-confidence. It could be that the rat represents time gnawing away unknown at your life. You may wake up one day to find your life empty."

"A cheery thought indeed."

Over the years, our therapy sessions were at times revealing but not what I would call enlightening. Finally, out of desperation, Doctor Helga suggested that there was a movie I needed to see. "Villard" she intoned, her Teutonic accent suddenly emerging.

"Villard, never heard of it."

"Yes, Villard, It's about vats."

Now that my therapist was returning to her linguistic "voots," I could see she was becoming increasingly more exasperated and curt with me. I did agree to see *Willard*, a favorite cult horror movie for rat lovers, but only with the stipulation that Helga would accompany me. Rather than being a therapeutic comfort, Helga irked me with her insensitive behavior. She had the audacity to sit there serenely munching on popcorn like she was watching a Mary Poppins movie, completely ignoring her traumatized patient whose stomach was churning, his shirt drenched in sweat, and breathing strained as the rats menacingly attacked people. I had to avert my eyes in pretty much every scene that highlighted Willard and his merry bands of rodents . I grabbed Helga's hand and squeezed it for support during the scariest scenes. All Helga could offer me for encouragement was some Milk Duds. In the end *Willard* only served to increase my rat nightmares. It was also creepy to discover that the director filmed the attack scenes by smearing peanut butter on the victims.

Doctor Helga and I mutually agreed to end the therapy, both

frustrated that I was progressing, if you could call it that, at a snail's pace. However, years later I did receive a call from her. She was raving about a recent movie she had seen, *Ratatouille*, that chronicled the experiences of a sophisticated rat who became a chef in a Paris restaurant. Helga urged me to go see it. She probably figured I could handle a lighthearted Disney animation better than the horror film disaster she subjected me to from our bygone therapy days. After summoning up the courage and reading many positive reviews, I forced myself to go to my local movie theatre. I loved the movie. It changed how I felt. Rats now seemed less demonic, but a movie could hardly resolve my psychosis.

Many years later, over five decades since my traumatic dream, I was visiting my lovely, hospitable sister-in-law, Cathleen, one summer in San Francisco. She lives in an exclusive neighborhood called Saint Francis Wood. Unfortunately, the area is shrouded in the fog belt. A leisurely walk on a July evening can mean donning a down jacket for the bone-chilling cold and then at bedtime adding a warm blanket for a comfortable night's sleep.

When people move into this wealthy neighborhood, it is not unusual for them to gut a perfectly fine house and renovate it to their liking. During my visit, a house down the street was undergoing such a renovation. It so happens that Cathleen has a pet cat named Precious. I could only think of Gollum in *Lord of the Rings* frantically searching for "My Precious." Anyway, Precious has a cat door that allows her to come and go as she pleases. Like most pet owners, Cathleen had a blind spot for her cat's conduct: minimizing, overlooking, and excusing behaviors that the small minority of people without pets find dangerous, unhygienic, or in some other way annoying. Cathleen is extremely fastidious in how neat she keeps the house, to the point that she sweeps her kitchen five times a day in constant vigilance lest one tiny crumb might somehow escape her sentry-like watch. Born into a family of ten girls who are no slouches when it comes to cleanliness and orderliness,

Cathleen has rather impressively maintained her ranking, year after year, as the family's number one neat freak.

So somehow, it is in no way contradictory to Cathleen's cleanliness philosophy that it is entirely acceptable for Precious to shed her cat hair on beds, sofas, and chairs without restraint or monitoring, and that family members who suffer from cat allergies must be subjected to life in a toxic environment and suffer, no relief in sight.  Well, simply, the little princess Precious rules, and poor Cathleen is blind to viewing this out-of-control feline with even a modicum of objectivity!

Naturally, with all the renovating activity in the neighborhood, the rats became uprooted.  So just before my visit, Precious discovered a new nocturnal hunting ground that began to put in motion the events that would lead to a  possible resolution of my persistent phobia.

When I arrived, Cathleen blithely told me the following story, the pet owner's blind spot completely in play.  "Oh John, it was just so adorable that Precious would want to show off her hunting prowess by bringing me her prized rat ."

"Do you feel the same way when a baby finch or cute little rabbit appears dismembered on your doorstep?"

"Well, no, but you should have seen the look on Precious' face when she put the rat down and it scurried off:  a sweet look of utter surprise.  I guess the rat was playing possum."

"Where's the rat now?"

"We have no idea.  For all we know it could still be somewhere in the house."

"Have you thought about sealing off her entrance door so Precious could become an outdoor cat?"  I asked, the pit of my stomach now in knots.

"Oh no, John, it would be too dangerous for my dear Precious to be out all night with so many ferocious cats living in this neighborhood."

I was aghast that Cathleen was taking everything so lightly, and I was concerned, very concerned, that a rat, potentially with bubonic plague, was roaming the hallways and probably setting up a staging area in the underbelly of the pipes and air ducts in the basement. I dreaded and feared the likely nightly forays into the living quarters upstairs.

That night, I was trying to fall asleep in the guest room, but for some reason I was tossing and turning, breaking out in a sweat which was incongruous since the night-time temperature was so cool and I needed plenty of covers to keep warm. Something just didn't feel right. When I woke in the morning after a very fitful night of sleep, I began to make the bed and when I turned over one of the blankets, there it was, a decapitated rat. I immediately flashed on the riveting scene in the movie, *The Godfather*, when Jack Woltz, the producer who refused to cast Johnny Fontane in a war film, awoke to discover the head of his prized thoroughbred, Khartoum, inside his covers at the foot of his bed. I got the opposite: the torso instead of the head!

I raced out of the room and yelled up to Cathleen, "There's a dead rat in my bed," feeling utterly violated and disgusted. Cathleen pretended to be sympathetic and concerned.

"Oh dear, I never know what's next with my unpredictable Precious," she observed, suppressing a laugh.

I was incredulous that Cathleen was dismissing this shocking incident as no more than Precious being Precious!

After a few days, the trauma of sleeping with a dead rat subsided. After all these years, the dream actualized itself. The dream had become reality; there WAS a rat in my bed. I felt like Dorothy and her friends. The Wizard of Oz had been revealed and exposed. He was like the rat, a grand illusion, and in the end had no real substance.  I had to sleep with the rat to kill it.  In other words, I had to endure the dead rat in my bed to kill my fear.  The dream was about reconciling the two worlds of my inner and outer life, but I needed to see the whole event through. It basically took a lifetime to do this.

When I look back on the original incident, I realize that I never clearly saw the end result of what happened when my father chopped down on that rat with his meat cleaver so many years before.  Until I threw back the blanket and saw a real decapitated rat, and not a figment of my imagination, my ordeal continued.  I wish I had been out there in the snow that day next to my brother Drew, witnessing up close a necessary exercise in exterminating vermin that were invading our living space.

If I had been counseled and talked through it a bit, perhaps I could have seen then and there the ordinary, mundane normalcy of what my father had to do.  Then the fear-and-terror- based nightmares, as well as that huge bump on the forehead, could have been avoided.

I had one final task to give closure to this disturbing ordeal that had now been mercifully resolved.  I called Helga, who was retired and living in a rest home in the Swiss Alps.   I brought her up to speed with all that had transpired.

"Just vonderful, John, just vonderful."

# Busted

"Ah ha, we have some pot smokers."

Not words we wanted to hear as the Middletown, New Jersey police officers, or the pigs as we preferred to call them back in 1970, suddenly appeared tapping on the car window. It was Labor Day weekend, and five acquaintances and I were sitting in a car with the windows rolled up just as the cops arrived to break up the noisy party we had been attending nearby. Quickly realizing that our arrest was imminent our two friends in the front seat immediately bolted from the car, and the cops gave chase. They were gone what seemed an eternity, and I was now at the threshold of the open car door with my friends urging me to take off. I weighed my options but dreaded the idea of running into a cop or getting shot, which was a legitimate concern. This was Middletown, New Jersey, and the police force was very reactionary. They had the county SWAT team for an area that did not have riots or hostage situations. And they were big time anti-drug. Even marijuana was viewed as a potential scourge of the community. The cops were not happy when they returned. One of us had thrown the paraphernalia, i.e. the pipe, into the weeds. They were quite aggressive as they threw us up against the police car for a pat down search.

Backup arrived to take all four of us to the police station. The police were intent on finding out who the other two guys were. They never read us our Miranda rights, instead threatening us with a high bail and serious drug offenses. The official charges were possession and under the influence of a controlled substance which was a misdemeanor. We probably had only a thimble-full of pot in our possession. If we had been really savvy and our parents not so uptight, we would have pleaded innocent and the test to prove it actually was marijuana would have consumed the minute amount of evidence, leading to the dismissal of charges.

It was now very late on the Saturday night of Labor Day weekend as we posed for mug shots and the detectives shined flashlights in our eyes, trying to see how stoned we were and hoping they had caught some dealers or lucked into an illicit drug ring.

All our belongings including wallets, rings, watches, and even our belts and sneaker laces were confiscated and put into large envelopes. Bail was set at one thousand dollars, and off we were escorted to our individual jail cells. It isn't what I would call a bucket list item, but everyone should have the experience of spending a night in jail. The threat of getting locked up for an extended period sent a shiver down my spine. I know it doesn't work as a deterrent, but it did make a strong impression of how we can take our freedom for granted until we waver a bit from law-abiding and then end up in the slammer. We tried to make light of the situation, but looming on the horizon was the dreaded phone call we would soon have to make.

"Look fellas, we've got toilets. They may have taken our belts and shoelaces but we can still drown ourselves."

That got a big laugh from my fellow prisoners. Then we were informed that we had the right to make one phone call. Of course none of us knew anybody other than our parents who could bail us out. I told my friends I was ready to make the call. I pretended I was on the phone.

"Is this Sal's? I'd like to order a large anchovy pizza with everything on it."

After the laughter died down, the heavy gravity of a call home, knowing my father would answer and how furious he would be, set in. I decided it was best to blurt out the bad news in short and direct Hemingway-like declarative sentences.

"Dad, it's Johnny. I'm at the Middletown Police Station. I've been arrested for marijuana. The bail is a thousand dollars."

"What?" my suddenly wide-awake father barked into the phone. He sounded like an angry pitbull. "I don't have that kind of money."

Of course, he didn't need it. That was just a ploy by the police to make sure our parents knew about our arrest. We were eventually released into their personal recognizance.

After the phone calls, we became much more somber as now we were going to have to face our agitated parents. A surreal scene unfolded when they arrived.

There we were, each in his own jail cell, when our parents first set eyes upon us. They were so distraught they might as well have been at the morgue identifying our lifeless bodies after a car wreck. Their privileged, white, private-school-educated sons were now would-be criminals facing serious misdemeanor charges for possessing a thimble-full of marijuana. Truly a fate worse than death.

To us it was like the scene from *The Adventures of Tom Sawyers* in which Tom and Huck attend their own funeral, hiding in the balcony. To complicate matters, all four of us were scheduled to leave for Boston the following week to begin our freshman year at the same college.

When we got home that night, my father and I sat down to talk even though it quickly became a one-sided conversation. He lit into me about the seriousness of the charges and what a blow it was to my future with the possible criminal record I would have. The fact that we were sitting down and having a conversation was new for me. I had never gotten this kind of attention before. Getting arrested evidently granted me "person of interest" status. He never sat me down and had any conversation of substance with me about the challenges of growing up or anything else. Sadly, and it may have to do partially with the fact that I was one of seven children, I had no history with my father.

Dad had been a heavy smoker but had quit a few months before.

Ironically, my "smoking" had led to him picking up his smoking addiction again that night. I can still see him in his white boxer shorts and matching white tee shirt lighting up a cigarette as we sat in the living room at what was then about four in the morning. He went on and on, railing about my questionable future. At one point he said disdainfully, "and you call yourself an athlete." I had been recruited to play on the tennis team at my would-be school, Boston College.

Now knowing that the other three arrested dope fiends were also attending Boston College, he immediately starting talking about bad influences, and how it would probably be best if I stayed at home and attended  Brookdale Community College or stayed in New Jersey and attended Rutgers.

But what really bothered my father most was that I didn't think smoking pot was any big deal.  He, on the other hand, was convinced it was a gateway drug leading swiftly to heroin addiction.  I was so blasé about it that Dad thought I was still under the influence.  It was becoming clearer and clearer by the time I went to bed around dawn that there was a huge gulf between us.  My lasting conclusion at the end of the night was how little I really knew my father.

When my devoutly Catholic mother awoke my two younger brothers, Billy and Robbie, the next morning, she greeted them with, "We have to pray for Johnny." No explanation. No news of what happened.  My brothers assumed I was dead, probably killed in a car crash.  It's a wonder how some parents think they are protecting their children by sparing them bad news, thinking they can't handle it.  Actually, children are better off being told bad news because they live on the vibe and emotional level and can feel how upset everyone is.

My father, who had never had a discussion with any of us about drugs, sex, or anything else of substance, polled my four older siblings to see if they had ever smoked pot.  Three of the four had.  He immediately demanded that they stop. They refused to do so.

Dad had a close family friend, Father Moore, a Roman Catholic priest who ran a reform school for delinquent teenage boys, and asked him to speak with me. Father Moore had seen every behavior under the sun and wasn't fazed that I was smoking a little pot. He asked me about my usage and if I was using other drugs. (I wasn't.)  When he reported back to my father that it wasn't a big deal, and that smoking pot wasn't that unusual or inherently evil, my dad was again furious. Dad was a high-powered business executive and a former FBI agent. He had enlisted in the Marines and served in the Pacific in World War II. He was a patent lawyer who worked in the Truman administration and was the point-man for big corporations in acquisitions of smaller companies in the 1960's and 70's which was the precursor to the mega-takeovers in the 80's.

He commuted by train everyday from Red Bank, New Jersey into New York City. It was about a four-hour round-trip.  Dad would leave the house around 6:30 everyday and not return until 7:30 at night. During the weekdays, he didn't have much time for anything more than a drink or two with Mom, a late dinner, and falling asleep in front of the TV. His seven children would parade by for greetings and quick updates on the day's highlights. He rarely attended any of our Little League games or any school activities. With his work schedule, we understood.

As a man of that generation, Dad expressed his love for his family by being the great provider, expecting Mom to hold up the home front. He was a great believer in Catholic schools, sending all seven of his children to Catholic high schools and colleges and footing the bill for all of us. I guess that's where he thought his obligation as a parent ended.

On the weekends, he played golf and was a fanatic about playing every Saturday and Sunday.

"It's my way of relaxing," he once told me. That was perfectly understandable given the nature of his high-pressure job and taxing schedule which entailed not only his grueling commute, but quite a bit of long-distance plane travel to Europe and Asia. What wasn't so understandable was his inability to balance his recreational needs with his family obligations.

Back in that era, a day at the club included 18 holes of golf with caddies, a few  rounds of drinks, and various card games like gin rummy and poker, with the losers from the golf matches intent on winning their money back at the card table.

On a typical Saturday, Dad would leave at 8:30, and we wouldn't see him again until 4:30 or 5:00. Mom became a complete golf widow, and we seven kids never spent much meaningful time with our father. He never took us fishing, played catch or in any way became involved in our lives unless there was some exceptional situation. An outstanding report card might elicit  a "good job" or misbehavior a dressing down as a result of Mom following through on her time-honored threat to "wait until your father gets home."  He had five sons and never was a role model for us other than his work ethic. No wonder the night I got busted I was wondering who this stranger was that was masquerading as my father.

Of course, my father was able to hire the right lawyer to plea bargain the misdemeanor charges against us. The District Attorney agreed to drop the drug charge, and we pleaded guilty to a disorderly person's charge, "Failure to Give a Good Account of Ourselves."  On any given day or period of our lives, we often joked, we could still plead guilty to that charge.

One Christmas Eve a few years later Dad announced at the breakfast table, "I'm going to play golf today."

It was a relatively warm day for late December, and Dad was fanatical enough to play despite the patches of snow scattered throughout the course. Bright orange Day-Glo colored golf balls was his solution to the white landscape he would be facing.

There was armed insurrection. We were older now, in our late teens and twenties, and we were not having it. He was met with a chorus:

"No way."

"That's bullshit."

"You've gotta be kidding!"

"On Christmas Eve?"

Dad was livid. He didn't expect this. We were ending his dereliction of duty once and for all. We called him out and so shamed him that he actually didn't go play golf on a special day reserved for family togetherness. We all wish we had done that years ago, but we were just too little, too afraid, and too unaware of what we were missing.

My siblings and I will all agree that to some extent Dad was a product of his time and we weren't the only big family with a distant father who potentially could have been a real patriarch. That didn't excuse his misplaced priorities. There are compromises he could have made.

But to be fair to Dad I must acknowledge his family history and be empathetic to the admirable job he did surviving his extremely self-centered mother. She apparently believed it was OK to play favorites with her first born son and reject her other two children. She adored her son Matt and called him by his given name. The others were referenced only by their relationship to their older brother. Dad was called "Brother" and my aunt was known as "Sissy." Grandma never addressed my future father or aunt by their given names. If that doesn't say it all! Probably one of the worse things a mother could do. No wonder Dad was emotionally unavailable. Actually in the big picture Dad overcame a lot to be as well-adjusted as he was. However, he wasn't equipped, given his history, to father seven needy children. Perhaps, if Catholics in that era had a better grasp of birth control, he could have managed to better fulfill his role with a much smaller family.

We do, however, have to give him a perverse credit.  Dad became an inadvertent inspiration for his five sons.   His poor example had us vowing that we would not be derelict in raising our own children.   We were adamant that we would become caring, hands- on, available fathers.  And we are.   We are not strangers to our children, and we participated in their lives when they were younger.  Dad showed us that without shared experiences and time spent together, there is no meaningful relationship.

In the end, I had to get busted to clearly see the remote unavailable father I actually had.  It was only then, after exposing what a stranger Dad was, that my siblings and I could "bust" him on that fateful family day, Christmas Eve.   There was no white Christmas that year, just a lesson in the meaning of true giving.

It was too late to revisit our childhoods.  We came to see that Dad did the best he could and that he had overcome plenty from his upbringing.  But we made damn sure in raising our own children that "the sins of the father would not be visited upon his sons."

# Kidney Stones

Am I the only person in medical history ever to catch kidney stones over the telephone? Back in the 1980's when I was in my mid-thirties and living in San Francisco, I received a call from my brother Bill in New York informing me that he had blood in his urine and had made an appointment to see a urologist.  I was concerned but didn't think much of it until about a week later when I too noticed an alarming red hue in my urine.  Bill was incredulous when I told him.   He had been diagnosed with kidney stones and now I was facing having them as well. Predictably I had to take quite a bit of ribbing from my other siblings who said I was way too impressionable and suffering from some strange case of sympathetic hypochondria.

I also made an appointment, and not surprisingly, the urologist recommended a battery of tests.

"It's a game of elimination," Dr. Prasad informed me in his clinical monotone.

"You could have a urinary tract infection, a kidney infection, kidney stones, kidney disease,  bladder cancer, or this could even be the result of strenuous exercise.   So I will need to test for a number of possible causes."

Dr. Prasad wanted to eliminate the possibility of bladder cancer.  The first test would be the ghastly cystoscopy, often described as the scariest test in all of medicine.  Performed without anesthesia, a tube is fitted with a tiny camera and  then pushed into the male body's tiny and most hyper-sensitive orifice, continuing up through the urethra to closely examine the bladder.

Nowadays doctors use flex scopes, but back in the eighties both my brother and I were subjected to the old "iron bar."  It was excruciating but at least I was temporarily reassured when my doctor said that I would only have some "minor" discomfort when I urinated the first time. I had plenty of time to ponder this as he left me alone in the examining room with my thoughts and a gauze bandage held on by a clamp on my privates. The acute pain indicated just how much I had been ripped to shreds.

I started thinking, Hmm, here I am in San Francisco. What if there's an earthquake? The rescuers digging through the rubble would find me barely alive with that clamp on my thing. I can just hear it. "What was this pervert doing?"

My wife, Colleen, was in the waiting room when I finally came out. She laughed nervously when she saw this pale figure emerge. I must have looked as if all of the blood had been drained from my body. Even though both my legs were in working order, I was noticeably limping. Colleen kissed me sympathetically and held me up by the arm as we made our way out to the parking lot.

We decided to go to the Tassajara Bakery for tea and their other-worldly poppy seed cake. This was nice and all, but I was already dreading that first pee. I braced myself for an experience that I was beginning to sense would be more than "minor discomfort." When we got home, I had to go real bad but I couldn't get the normal reflex to work. It was just too painful to go. Finally, I drew the hottest bath I could tolerate and was able to urinate in the water. It remained excruciating for about five days. So much for "minor discomfort."

No cancer, but an x-ray did reveal that I had a huge stone lodged in my kidneys. Stones occur when minerals and other substances in the blood crystallize in the kidneys, forming masses or stones. These stones may consist of small, sharp-edged crystals or smoother, heavier formations that resemble polished river rocks. If they are small enough, they usually exit the body naturally during urination and will go unnoticed. In my case, the process of liquid waste leaving the body was disturbed by an accumulation of sediment in the kidneys. Due to a genetic predisposition, pockets or cul-de-sacs formed and then became depositories for the grains that would normally pass to the ureter, bladder, and then out. Thus the conditions were ripe for creating stones.

After a bit of discussion, it was decided that a lithotripsy was the best option. Lithotripsy uses sound waves to break up large kidney stones into smaller pieces. Being non-invasive, it quickly replaced surgery as the treatment of choice. It was a new procedure, only a few years old when it was recommended that I have it done.

Dressed in what appeared to be some sort of hospital boxers, I was lowered on to a seat that hovered out over a pool of water. Before the anesthesia took effect I remember feeling like both the carnival clown at the dunking booth and the repentant sinner about to undergo a total immersion baptism in the River Jordan. When I regained consciousness in the recovery room, my lower back and kidney area were quite sore and black and blue. It felt as if I had been taken into a dark alley and beaten with a two-by-four.

The urologist came to my hospital room a short while later to check on me. After a few cursory pleasantries and a check on my condition, he said somewhat sternly, "It's important that you urinate now to flush out your kidneys."

"Sorry, Doctor, but I'm in no condition to do that right now."

"Alright then, I'll have to perform another cystoscopy." When I heard those threatening words I catapulted out of my hospital bed as if it were spring loaded and dragged the IV stand with me into the bathroom. I peed a stream of one hundred percent dark red blood which normally would have set off alarm bells but now didn't faze me in the least. I had avoided what my brother and I had come to call "the test." We both vowed we would never again subject ourselves to such excruciating pain. I was fully prepared to say to any doctor then and in the future that I would play the odds that I didn't have bladder cancer. I was grateful for the full life that I had already led and was at peace with my Maker. I was never again having a TV camera shoved up that impossibly small opening. The next morning, Dr. Prasad came to check on me and give me the OK for discharge from the hospital. He told me that now that the lithotripsy was a success and the stone had been pulverized, I would be passing some debris or "gravel" as he called it. He even gave me a strainer so that any of these tiny particles I passed could then be analyzed to determine what type of stone had been forming in my kidneys. He would make possible dietary recommendations from there. What he didn't tell me is that one man's gravel is another man's boulder. Once again I had become a victim of medical minimizing.

Passing the "gravel" became an ordeal of major proportions. Each piece of debris had to make its way from the kidneys down the narrow pathway designed for liquid waste. I was passing stones of the jagged edge variety, not smooth gravel particles. Each episode entailed writhing on the floor in fetal position, and then instant relief as the stone passed into the strainer which I jockeyed into position like a group of fireman adjusting their rescue net for someone about to jump from a burning building.

This is as close as we men will ever get to the experience of bringing a child into this world and the only ammo we can possibly use in our "been there argument" when trying to counter female accounts of child birth pain. "So you've had three children. Big deal, I've had thirty-eight!"

Be it childbirth, running marathons, or passing kidney stones, if not for the memory mechanism that allows us to forget pain, we'd be living in a childless world of short distance walkers in which kidney stone operations were more common than hip replacements.

It's mind boggling to know that a kidney stone can range in size from a grain of sand to a pearl to a golf ball. My stone was the size of a marble and the most common variety, calcium oxalate.  There are many theories as to what one can do to prevent stones from reoccurring.  Changing diet by limiting sodium and foods with oxalate , especially rhubarb (stick with apple pie!) as well as calcium/dairy products doesn't produce the desired results.  The problem isn't over-consumption but the inability of the kidneys to process these minerals properly.  Cranberry juice is no panacea either.  What seems to work is water, lots of it.  I drank two and a half gallons a day to help flush out the gravel, literally floating through the experience.

Kidney stones above all else are mysterious.  Like Halley's Comet, they suddenly appear then disappear.  Most people have kidney stone attacks between the ages of forty and fifty.  For some it's a one-time event, but once a person has a second occurrence of stones, it is  likely that more will follow.

Bill and I will be forever bonded over our vow to never again undergo the gruesome cystoscopy.  I feel bad that my poor brother suffered through a botched lithotripsy and has been doomed to recurring stones unlike my (knock on wood) one-time experience.  I suppose, and I don't want to be too harsh here, but it does seem easy to conclude that it serves him right for giving me kidney stones over the phone.

# Birth Day

The best we can do as men is press our faces up against the fishbowl. We never get inside to swim in the ocean of life like women do . Women live in rhythm while men become philosophers and pontificate about how to live life.  To women, men at best can be contributors, but to experience gestation and bring a precious new soul into the world?  Not possible.  It is through the whole pregnancy-birth process that a man gets to see how much of an outsider he really is...

My wife, Colleen, was about to give birth any day.  She was at full term on this Sunday, November 18, 1990.  She experienced that odd precursor to labor-a burst of energy that manifested in a three mile round trip walk to the indoor pool and a forty-five minute swim.  Shouldn't evolution have the expectant mother more in rest-up mode for the tremendous  expenditure of energy that it would soon take to bring new life into the world?  Not so, just one of many baffling behaviors that leave us as men just shaking our heads.

So a few hours after her swim, Colleen calmly announced, "Call the doctor.  I'm having contractions."  The obstetrician wanted to know how far apart the contractions were.

"Every 10-15 minutes."

"Bring her in right away.  I'll meet you there."  I grabbed her suitcase and asked if she needed anything else.

"Get the car, Stupid."

I did.  "Do you need any help getting in?"

"No, I can walk, Stupid."

Colleen had described a number of my actions and behaviors in the past as stupid, but she had never addressed me as "Stupid" before, so I was taken aback by this strange and unexpected moniker.  I dismissed it as part of the labor that was now beginning to take over. However, I was admittedly concerned about stories I had heard of birthing mothers cursing out their husbands and about the potential "F- bombs" that could be directed my way during the actual birth.

As we headed off to the hospital, we fell into an awkward silence. It felt like a blind date gone awry. Even making small talk with this sudden stranger was challenging. My mind raced frantically. "How do you feel, honey?" No, can't ask that. I'll get slammed. "Do you think we'll make it in time?" No, another dumb question. "Warm day for November, isn't it, Colleen?" No, she wouldn't appreciate that either.

So we traveled along in silence except for Colleen's gasps that were resounding like clockwork. Unlike the blind date, I couldn't just take her home. We had a whole life-changing ordeal to experience ahead of us.

By the time we arrived at the Wayne County Hospital in rural Honesdale, Pennsylvania, Colleen was in full labor as the contractions were coming much more frequently. I pulled right up to the front entrance.

"What should I do with the car?"

"Park it, Stupid."

No time for that. I abandoned it right there. We went right up the elevator and burst into the maternity ward. We were about to have our baby. The obstetrician, Dr. Yoo, had confidently told Colleen that because there was a ten year gap between the birth of her first child from a previous marriage and this pregnancy, she could expect to experience the same duration of labor of a woman giving birth for the first time (anywhere from 8-20 hours). What he didn't know was that Colleen was an amateur opera singer possessing super-strong abdominal muscles as well as being an expert in diaphragmatic breathing. Her kegels were strong and flexible, too.

Men have no idea what kegels are.  It was only because I once took a Pilates class with all women  that I knew.  The instructor was going on and on about how certain postures benefited the kegels.  I asked her after class what they were.  She laughed and said guys always asked her that.  Kegels are the pelvic floor muscles.  I gather strong ones help support the uterus.

When we entered, Doctor Yoo and two nurses were lounging around, not expecting Colleen to be so close to giving birth.  They immediately rushed off to put on their scrubs.

Colleen's water broke.  Still no sign of the doctor or nurses.  I could only think of what they would do in the movies:  boil some water.

Colleen lay down on the bed. She began to groan and gasp for air.  What was taking the doctor so long? I suddenly saw something emerging.  It was very dark in color.  Holy Jesus, was that the meconium?  Now I was really confused.  How could the baby's first bowel movement lead the way?  Whoa, what's going on?  No, it was Kevin's head.  He's got dark hair.  Finally just seconds before I was about to deliver, or better yet catch our baby, the nurses and doctor arrived.

I got myself under enough control to welcome our newborn with a "Hi Kev," but I never had an opportunity to coach Colleen in the La Maze breathing techniques we learned in our child birth classes.  But let's face it, these classes only promote feel-good activities that pretend that the husband can be somehow involved in the childbirth process.   In the heat of the battle, if I had tried, "Breathe darling, breathe.  Push, breathe," I swear Colleen would have risen from her hospital bed and beaten me to a pulp.  Yet when it was all over, she did say how much she appreciated my being there to support her.  And I was more than happy to embrace my cheerleader role from the sidelines.  Still, all new dads will readily admit that we are not  innocent bystanders.  We know that we have made a major contribution to the pain our wives endure, but at the same time, we are helpless to really do anything about it.

So there was our boy Kevin. I felt both joyous and relieved. After the doctor checked out his vital signs, the nurse asked Colleen if she would like to hold him. Colleen opened her arms so lovingly and tenderly that I was moved to tears as I watched her embrace our tiny son. She cradled him delicately just below her neck. They both looked so angelic, the ideal picture of mother and child, just as I had imagined it all along.

# Barbershops USA

Everywhere we look, our institutions are crumbling. Governments, churches, schools, and even the family are under tremendous stress nowadays. The barbershop seems to have weathered this storm as a functional social center and as a reliable anchor, no matter the changes in style or fashion. Barbers know their job is to be adaptable and to cut hair in whatever style the client wants, be that to conform to the current craze or to make a statement. With all the turmoil in society, plenty of barbershops fulfill the traditional role of adding vitality and function to Main Street. They also provide continuity and a welcome refuge from the dizzying changes society is undergoing. No surprise that "classic barbershops" are common nowadays.

I lived for quite a number of years in Honesdale, Pennsylvania, in the northeastern part of the state. Like many rural areas of this country, it is family-oriented, conservative, and tradition-minded. Micki's Barbershop on Main Street reflects those values as the owner Micki Theobold prides herself on "modern barbering techniques in a clean, comfortable, classic atmosphere."

Micki is the fourth generation of a family business that opened in 1890. She learned the trade from her father and uncle. As they aged and eventually retired, the daughter who swept hair as a kid and loved to hang out at the shop with her father, took over. In 2004, she closed "Theobold's" for renovations and gutted the shop. In addition to wide plank wood floors and wainscoting, Micki installed traditional old barber chairs. She then reopened as "Micki's Classic Barbershop" with a look that is now very much in vogue as it harkens back to a time in America when craft was highly valued. She then began training and hiring female barbers. Today, each of the four barber chairs is "manned" by a woman.

I took my son Kevin for his first haircut when he was about two years old. We had no idea at the time that Kevin was beginning a streak at Micki's that would last for nearly seventeen years.  Father and son, we went together for our haircuts.  It was male bonding as well as a comforting ritual.  The barbers got to know Kevin and watched him grow up.  And Kevin's musical horizons were expanded, as he was a captive audience to the constant background music from bygone eras:  Glenn Miller, Frank Sinatra, Frankie Valli, and lots of oldies from the 50's.

One of the time-honored techniques that Micki resurrected from previous generations was the back of the neck shave with hot lather and a straight-edge razor.  No electric razor leaves the back of your neck feeling so smooth and groomed.   After all, it's the overgrown neck hair that begins to feel too much like fur, that signals most men that it is time to get a haircut.  Once a man becomes accustomed to this pleasing signature to his barbering experience there is no turning back.

When Kevin turned twelve, he received his first neck shave.  He remembers it as a rite of passage signifying that he was no longer a little kid.  I can still remember him repeatedly stroking the back of his neck and exclaiming to me, "Dad it's so smooth. It's so smooth!"

"That's right son.  Welcome to the club."

Once established with a barber that understands the traditions of a classic haircut, a strong bond of loyalty develops.  Unlike in baseball, there are no away games.  If you must be out of town for a while,  you get a haircut before you depart.  You cannot leave this important ritual to any old barber on the road.  When we moved away across the state line into New York, we still made the trek to Micki's, like homing pigeons returning to roost.

Just like Cal Ripkin, the Baltimore Orioles shortstop who holds the Major League record for  consecutive games played in baseball, Kevin's longevity streak was tested.  Cal had to play through injuries and  later, the criticism that he was putting the streak before the younger players who were ready to replace him. Kevin's dilemma was visiting his cousins for extended periods during vacations. His streak ended unceremoniously at a chain salon in a strip mall in suburban Maryland. I'll never forget when we commiserated together. "God, Dad. They only used scissors," he said incredulously.

As time went on, Kevin went off to college at Penn State and began to get haircuts there at the university, but still loved to return to Micki's when he was home. I faithfully continued my interstate journeys, migrating back to Honesdale every six week like a Canadian goose who instinctively knows it is time to fly south in autumn. After Kevin graduated and I retired, we both were facing the dreaded challenge of finding acceptable barbers in our new locales. Kevin moved to Brooklyn, New York to join his fellow millennials and look for a job. And I was off to Santa Fe, New Mexico.

In Brooklyn Kevin moved to the Bedford Stuyvesant neighborhood. Like many of his generation he lives in an apartment with a couple of roommates to reduce the exorbitant city rents. Kevin has become a patron of KZ&C, the local barber shop on Thompkins Street.

He bonded right away with the owner, Brett, a native of Trinidad who, like Kevin, is a rabid Knicks fan. They immediately began passionate discussions of what the Knicks need to do to become a playoff team.

In Kevin's neighborhood the barbershop is still a social center. Men who are in no need of a haircut will gather to discuss the topics of the day. The shop often appears crowded with customers, but half the men are there only to hang out and socialize.

Brett, and only Brett, cuts Kevin's hair. His choices are a "shape up," a "regular," or a "kids' haircut." Kevin has decided to keep his hair much shorter which seems to work better for an electric razor cut. The other two barbers rent their chairs from Brett and bring in their own customers. There are no random haircuts. You go to your guy.

KZ&C is open long hours, from 11:00 in the morning to 10:00 at night. Kevin passes the shop on his way home. Some nights the patrons are gathered to watch a Knicks game, as the barber chairs become sought-after seats for viewing the game. He will stop in to get the lowdown. One night after another discouraging Knicks loss, Kevin was greeted by Brett. "Our boy didn't play well tonight." He was referring to Kristaps Porzingis the seven-foot three- inch power forward from Latvia who has been such a pleasant surprise, surpassing  expectations with his solid all-around play.

Now, I had to see if I could match Kevin's good fortune and find a suitable barbershop when I moved to Santa Fe.  I began my search concerned that I wouldn't be able to find an old-school barber who still gave neck shaves with the hot  lather and straight-edge razor. I figured the upscale places would be all scissors and trim.  My only realistic hope was that the prevalent  Latino barbers in the city had this tradition.  I Googled "barbershops Santa Fe" and there it was:  "Johnny's Classic Barber Shop." Since my family and friends call me Johnny, how perfect would it be to have my hair cut by a Johnny!  Most of the reviews were raves and I loved Johnny's statement on his website:  "In the days of our fathers, the corner barber shop was a place where a man could go and put aside the cares of the world for a while. He could relax and have his hair cut by a craftsman who took pride in his work.  That shop has largely been replaced by the generic salon in the mall.  But a few of us hold to the tradition of the golden age.  Classic barbering is still alive."

After my first haircut at Johnny's, I couldn't wait to call Kevin and compare notes.

"You're not going to believe the neck shave, Kev.  Johnny stores the hot towels in a rice cooker!  Wouldn't you love to hear a typical Japanese guy's take on this unique use of his nation's iconic kitchen appliance? And then he tops it off with a neck massage.  This is the best!   And yours?"

"Well, it's not that different, Dad.  The neck shaves here are about the edges being neat and  clean, just no hot lather or straight edged razor. But what I like most is I get to satisfy my basketball discussion fix each month, not to mention the fifteen-dollar charge, which for New York City is an extraordinary bargain."

"What about the music, Kev?"

"They play classic Hip Hop from the 80's and 90's among other stuff. It helps that I love all kinds of music. I really know early Hip Hop and can converse and hold my own in any discussion.   What does your guy play, Frank Sinatra?"

"Not quite, Kev.  How about Gregorian Chant!  It's actually the perfect choice.  Any concerns or preoccupations I may have just seem to drift away.  I don't know if there is a more perfectly soothing background serenade than this ancient church music!"

"Cool.  You know, it's funny Dad: all this emphasis on classic barbershops and returning to the golden age of barbering.  Well, many of the city neighborhood barbershops are classic, too.  The difference is that they've always been classic and still are.  They haven't changed anything. They were a social center back in the day and still are today."

Kevin and I had many more conversations comparing notes and discussing the various nuances of the two barbershop experiences.  There was so much more to tell him about "Classic Johnny."

Johnny works alone in a small room he has rented on the ground floor of an apartment complex.  He tried to work with other barbers earlier in his career but just couldn't keep up with the volume expectation.

"Johnny, you give excellent haircuts, but you're just too slow.  We're going to have to let you go," he was told by his last boss.

This was a blessing for Johnny as he was now free to work at his own pace. He will spend up to forty-five minutes giving a proper haircut. There is no dropping by, as his policy is appointment only. As it is, he struggles to keep up with his schedule. It would be way too stressful for Johnny and the customers if he were faced with a backlog. You see, Johnny is a perfectionist, an artist, a sculptor of hair. He prefers to work to completion without the client seeing the unfinished work. He then likes to spin the chair dramatically toward the mirror and unveil his finished product like an accomplished sculptor pulling the sheet off his newly- chiseled masterpiece.

I once asked Johnny what the breakdown was between clients that just leave the haircut in his hands as opposed to those who give specific directions.

"One camp, about twenty percent, basically don't say much and just trust me to give them a decent haircut. Some give vague directions like 'take some off the sides.' Then there are those who just don't care enough to give directions. I love working with this group because I can give them a haircut that fits their face and head shape."

This leaves Johnny free to be the Michelangelo of haircutting. Just like the great artist, he is given commissions, but prefers to be unencumbered to sculpt his " David" as he envisions it.

Now, the other eighty percent that Johnny gladly puts up with are usually younger, more vain, and more specific in what they want.

"But you know, that is very satisfying in its own way too. I love to see the client satisfaction and then hear the next time how much his girlfriend or wife loved it, or the positive comments he received at work."

Johnny has quite the flair for creating a relaxing and soothing environment that is eminently suitable for the haircut experience. The pictures on the wall of Johnny Cash, John F. Kennedy, Yul Brynner, Cary Grant, and Sophia Loren suggest a classic bygone era while various antiques, like razors from the golden age of barbering, placed around the room pay homage to the history. Johnny adds to this comforting environment by offering his patrons a free beer while getting their hair cut. He had special labels made up for the excellent local micro brew he provides. You can sit back, relax, and enjoy either a Pompadour Porter or a Flat Top Pale Ale.

The first time I had this delightful experience, I was naturally concerned about hair getting into the beer bottle.

"Johnny, is there a method to this?" I asked, concern in my voice.

" Yes." He answered without hesitation. "There are three. You can either put the bottle on the counter, keep it under the cape, or plug the bottle with your thumb."

I went with the thumb method, which worked perfectly and is the most popular choice of the clientele.

As I told Kevin, the perfect complement to this liquid refreshment is Johnny's inspired choice of music: Gregorian Chant. Johnny has been playing the same tape for almost five years now. Unlike songs from the past that we can wear out through too much repetition, like the Rolling Stones' "I Can't Get No Satisfaction" or some of the Beatles songs, Gregorian Chant has a way of staying new and timeless. It is the perfect backdrop to conversation or quiet reflection. This works perfectly as some clients want to close their eyes, rest, and let their attention be drawn inward while others are happy to engage Johnny in conversation. Either way, I know this: there is no other barbershop in the world that offers this sublimely-paired combination of exceptional beer and restorative Gregorian Chant!

I didn't get into the details with Kevin and accurately describe to him how Johnny has elevated the revered neck shave to an art form. He begins with a hot towel applied soothingly to the neck. He stores the towels in a rice cooker to keep the temperature just so. He applies the hot lather and then meticulously uses the straight-edged razor to gently shave the back of the neck. Next, he rubs on a tonic that smells very familiar and reminds me of haircuts as a young boy. The cherry on top is the restorative shoulder massage that acts as an exclamation point to this delightful haircut experience.

Johnny once told me about an older man whose hair he was cutting for the first time. When the neck shave commenced, the man started to cry. He hadn't had a neck shave in over fifty years. He was just flooded with emotion as this simple procedure evoked distant, heartfelt memories.

Johnny is a man who cares about his community. When he was in barber school, he decided to volunteer at the homeless shelter as a way to both hone his craft and be a positive force for the less fortunate. The staff was happy to have him provide this service to the residents.

It's a familiar story how guys end up in the shelter. They get buried by a perfect storm of negative events: they lose their jobs, can't pay the rent, begin drinking too much, and end up living in their cars. The next step is the homeless shelter. Johnny became a sign of hope to the residents as they tried to get back on their feet and become functioning members of society. He helped them look presentable to the world, specializing in the "interview haircut."

"When you're down on your luck like that, self-image really suffers. To be able to present yourself looking polished and confident, and holding your head high is huge. That's half the battle in a job interview."

The men would often return to thank Johnny and share the great news if they got the job. A few of the guys became a little too attached to him and asked to leave some of their stuff in his barbershop when he finally got his own place.

"I was OK with that at first, but I really had to put my foot down when they began using my shop as a homeless drop-in center."

Johnny knew he had done his part and that it was time for these guys to move on and face whatever fate had in store for them. He had a business to set up and build.

It didn't take long for Johnny to develop a loyal following. You might say a *fiercely* loyal following. He has been consistently ranked as the number one barbershop in Santa Fe. A number of years ago, a reporter from a weekly newspaper came in for a haircut. He had very long hair, and Johnny did his best, but after a few minutes, he announced he wasn't comfortable cutting hair that long and that, of course, there would be no charge. Not one word from the reporter until about three months later when he wrote a scathing review. He didn't mention the professional manner in which Johnny treated him, nor did he understand that a "classic haircut" is not "take a little off the shoulders." There was outrage among the true believers. The reporter actually received a death threat. This classic barbering is serious business...

And so, as Kevin planned to come to Santa Fe for a visit, I put the usual tourist destinations such as the Plaza, the art galleries of Canyon Road, and The San Miguel Mission on the back burner. We had a real "shrine" to visit: Johnny's Classic Barbershop.

# 4

# School Days

*In learning we teach and in teaching we learn.*

---Phil Collins


### Kindergarten

Kindergarteners love to give hugs often when you least expect it. This was one of the first lessons I learned when I first started working with them. Often times, a kid would run towards me, building up a head of steam as they charged to give me a hug. If I were talking to the teacher or in some other way distracted, and didn't see the student coming, I risked serious injury to the groin area as that was the typical five-year-old's hugging height. If the other kids saw this, it would sometimes unleash a copy-cat mob mentality in which ten or fifteen out of control kindergarteners were simultaneously taking a bead on me and moving toward me like the *Charge of the Light Brigade*. I had no choice but to be like a halfback in the open field, keeping a 360 degree awareness ready to gently stiff arm would-be huggers. If I were caught unaware, I risked not only painful injury but a sudden change in my speaking voice to high-pitched falsetto.

In 2009, the Monticello Central School District in Monticello, New York decided to change the configuration of its two elementary schools . The Cooke School, previously kindergarten through second grade, and the Rutherford School, previously third grade through fifth grade, would both become K-5 schools. The idea was to create more educational continuity for the students, eliminate the upheaval of changing schools, and make it easier for parents by having all their younger children in one building.

As the Assistant Principal at the Rutherford School, I had no experience working with kindergarteners. Would they understand our school message concerning responsibility and following the rules in the same way that had worked for the older children? I just didn't know.

I had worked with third to fifth graders for many years and knew what they were capable of academically and what to expect behaviorally. I had always especially marveled at the capabilities of third graders. In reading, they had progressed from decoding and phonics in the primary grades to reading for meaning and comprehension. They were beginning to reason in math and were embarking on learning their times tables. In art, they still possessed that innocence and child-like line quality in their drawing. Third grade has been called the beginning of the American high school. So true, because if by the end of the year the students are understanding what they are reading and have mastered basic math concepts, they are on their way. Yet, it was their constant enthusiasm for life and learning that I admired most. It was the end of their early childhood and the beginning of their independence as learners and their emergence into a more self-conscious social life.

The kindergarteners, however, were a mystery until we finally got to observe them in action. When they arrived that first day, some were crying and clinging to their mothers, while others marched in, ready to take on the new experience. They were the new recruits arriving at boot camp in varying degrees of readiness. Some had been in pre-school for a few years; others had no schooling. Some could already read while others didn't know how to hold a book right side up. This was a big step up from their pre-K experience. Now they were in the big leagues: full day, no naps, and a rigorous academic schedule.

People will often reference the book *Everything I Needed To Know I Learned In Kindergarten*. It's not that simple, nor is kindergarten that thorough. The learning curve is very steep, and the kids who get with the program are off to a great start. They come in as babies, and just like the recruits who arrive the first day at the Marine Corps base camp, they are unaware of what is really in store for them. We train these eager five-year-olds in the basics of reading, math, and socialization so they are prepared to take on the next step of challenges that lay ahead in their development. They are loyal, loving, and enthusiastic sponges who are not shy about expressing how they feel.

So, I spent time getting to know these dynamic five year olds, visiting classrooms and trying to demonstrate to them that I was accessible and would help them if something or someone was bothering them but at the same time, making it clear they would have to deal with me if they misbehaved. I slipped into classrooms and observed the kids learning and asked them questions to check their understanding.

I soon discovered how many kindergarteners have speech impediments. Thankfully they're not major and most of the kids will outgrow the impediment, but it seemed as if at least half the class had "Elmer Fudd Syndrome," that is, they couldn't pronounce the "r" sound, substituting "w" instead. So a rebound in basketball became a "webound." And a "Room with a View" became a "Womb with a View."

My surname, Correa, became fair game for this mispronunciation. Kindergarteners trying to get my attention would often shout out "Mr. Caweer, Mr Caweer." Once, I had to deal with a problem in the office and left my morning station in the hallway where I would greet students entering the building after they disembarked from the buses. Motor-mouth Patrick was not having it and came storming into the office.

"Mr. Caweer, Mr. Caweer. Why aren't you out in the hall? That's your job." So now I had to justify my job description to a five-year-old.

"Well, Patrick, I have other things to take care of, but I'll be there tomorrow."

Patrick took that that as an excuse and kept repeating "Mr. Caweer,

Mr. Caweer, it's your job."

Patrick, as I was learning, was representative of kindergarten thinking. If we were holding him accountable to line up, sit quietly on the carpet, and follow his teacher's directions, then "Mr Caweer" should demonstrate that he can be responsible too and not abandon his morning post.

In order to help make our school more user-friendly and more personal for the students, I would often invite kids to eat lunch with me in my office. As word got out that this option was available, it became a bit of a problem, as twenty-five to thirty students were begging to dine with me on any given day. I didn't fully understand the appeal, but I guess it had to do with feeling like they were being treated special.

One day, three adorable Latina kindergarteners, Claribel, Marissa, and Emelia appeared with their lunch trays at my office door, uninvited. How did they slip away from all the aides that were monitoring the lunch room? Kindergarteners have an uncanny knack for ditching supervision. That's why teachers constantly take a head-count anytime they move the class anywhere. If kindergarteners were prisoners at ADX, the super maximum-security prison in Colorado, it would only be a matter of time before all of them would be running around in the fields outside the prison playing tag and picking daisies, unbeknownst to the guards. One look at the girls' pleading faces and I couldn't turn them away. I said, "Sure, it's OK." So, in they came and sat down around my circular mediation table and began devouring their lunch of chicken nuggets, rice, salad, and a fruit cup. I heated up some leftovers in my microwave and joined them. What conversations can one have with five-year-olds? Well, I had a series of stock questions and conversation starters. Naturally, I would ask how they were doing in class and about their teacher. They said they were doing fine and their teacher was so nice. Next question, "Are you going to be ready for the first grade?"

Confidently shaking their heads up and down, the girls answered with an emphatic, "Yes."

Then, I would ask about their families and if they had any brothers or sisters. Invariably, they would have younger siblings.

"Do you help Mom take care of the little one?"

Yes, they would hold their baby brothers or sisters, feed them a bottle, and in some cases even change diapers although most mothers seem to spare them from this unpleasant task. Now, if the siblings were a bit older, about three, I would ask the following question: "Do you play school with them?"

I knew the inevitable answer was "Yes." If need be, the younger one was forced to play. The kindergartener played the teacher and the sibling always the student. No wonder girls run circles around boys in school. I've never heard of a boy fantasizing about being a teacher. They're too busy playing with toy guns and building things. Meanwhile, girls progress with their innate need for expression to keeping diaries and becoming would-be novelists and poets. A fair number of boys, on the other hand, are resisting reading and are such impatient writers that they think they're done after the first draft.

"Oh, by the way girls, I don't get it. Wouldn't you rather be in the cafeteria eating with the other students?"

"No, it's too noisy in there," said Claribel.

"Who's making all the noise? Noisy students like you... Just kidding."

So the next day, I was sitting in my office quietly catching up on some paper work when my three little friends appeared at my door with their lunch trays. Once again, they had masterminded another escape from the cafeteria. I rose from desk and went to the door to greet them.

"Hi girls, no, I can't have lunch with you today. There are 500 other students. It wouldn't be fair, would it? I need to give someone else a chance."

The girls ignored what I said, brushed by me, sat down at the table, and began to eat.

"No, really, girls."

They continued to ignore me. I realized I was helpless. There was no stopping them. They were having lunch in my office. I succumbed to their bold action and sat down and accepted the fact that I had no chance against these three determined kindergarteners who played me as if I were one of their younger brothers.

Hmm, I could see that these five-year-olds were making assumptions much more quickly than I expected. A third-grader would never return the next day expecting another special lunch. The kindergarteners evidently set patterns more quickly than upper elementary students. *OK, we had lunch with Mr. Correa today, so that means we can do it every day.*

Discipline is where my education in handling and understanding kindergarteners really began. Because they are only five years old, we treated them differently than the older students. It's more a learning process although accountability and responsibility are still central to behavioral expectations. We were trying to teach these little ones how to behave in a group. Some of them, due to lack of pre-school or negligent parenting, were like wild stallions that weren't going to allow a bit to be put in their mouths. They had a fit if they didn't get their way and would pinch, scratch, or bite if another kid didn't comply with their demands. We didn't punish them too severely. If they were out of sorts, we would remove them from class, take them down to the Principal's office, and have them sit in the "naughty chair." We would focus their attention on an hour glass to distract them from their wailing . After a few minutes of watching the sand fall down into the lower compartment, they would usually calm down enough so that we could talk to them, remind them of their responsibilities, ask them if we needed to call home, and then return them to class for an apology to the teacher and another chance to start over. Like all students, they wanted to avoid that call home at all costs. Usually, that was enough for most kids to turn it around, but of course there were the more challenging cases.

Mariah was sent down to the office by her teacher, Mrs. Mentnech. She had older siblings, so her first line of defense was to lie or to blame someone else. The note from her teacher said she was put out in the hall to take a time-out for being disruptive. Every time Mrs. Mentnech looked through the glass door to check on her, Mariah stuck her tongue out. I put Mariah on the hot seat (the naughty chair) to hear her side of the story.

"So Mariah, why were you sticking your tongue out at your teacher?" I asked.

"I wasn't. I was licking my lips," answered this savvy five year old without skipping a beat.

"Oh really, maybe you can explain this to your father when I call him."

"I didn't mean to do it." Then the flood of tears, sobbing, "but he'll spank me."

"Well, maybe I won't need to call him if you get down to your classroom, apologize to Mrs. Mentnech, and turn your behavior around. Do you think you can do that?"

"Yes, Mr. Caweer."

Hand-in-hand, we walked down the hall back to her classroom and had a brief conference in the hall with her teacher. I watched Mariah apologize and promise to turn things around. Later that day at dismissal, Mariah ran up to me and hugged me before she got on her bus.

"Good job today, Mariah. You turned it around and got back on track. I'll talk to Mrs. Mentnech and see if it's OK with her, but if you can behave and get your work done I'll let you and a friend come for lunch in the office."

It was vital that Mariah saw that if she took responsibility for her behavior and was willing to take corrective action, she would be forgiven and given another opportunity to prove to herself that she could behave. Equally important was to keep the relationship intact. I could be disappointed in Mariah's behavior but never wrote her off or labeled her as a bad kid. My job was to build trust and cultivate connections with kids, not to scare them. Then there was a chance that I could influence them.

We had lunch detention for students who were misbehaving or practicing work-avoidance. Instead of eating in the cafeteria with their classmates, they had to eat in the back of a classroom somewhere else in the building where the students hadn't had lunch yet or had returned from the cafeteria. After a while, even if their teacher made sure they had work to do while in the lunch detention classroom, the kids didn't seem to mind too much. Discipline procedures seem to wear out after time as they become the norm. The exception of course, is the naughty chair, which no kindergartener ever took for granted knowing a call home was imminent.

In order to up the ante, we sent kindergarteners to fifth-grade classrooms and vice versa. The students hated this. The fifth graders had to sit on those tiny chairs in the back of the room and listen to the teacher tell them how much better behaved her kindergarteners were, sitting on the carpet and being attentive. Often the teacher knew the fifth grader and would ream them out further with comments like, "still not getting your work done."

The kindergartners dreaded going to the fifth grade classes. These were the big kids, and there was a good chance a sibling or a cousin would be in one of the lunch detention classes. That could mean a possible ratting out to the family later as in "guess who visited my class today?" as part of the dinner table conversation. But worst of all was being sent to Mrs. Selkirk's class. She wasn't physically imposing , but she was one of those teachers who viewed herself as a teacher of all kids she came in contact with, whether they were assigned to her or not.

So, a kindergartener named Kyari couldn't get that pinching was unacceptable. I talked to her about it a few times, but then her teacher, Mrs. Amstead, and I decided she needed to pay a lunch detention visit to Mrs. Selkirk's class. Kyari, looking adorable with her copious hair piled atop her tiny head, was in tears as I brought her down to Mrs. Selkirk's.

"What's your name and why are you here?" boomed Mrs. Selkirk in a loud and displeased voice.

"Kyari, I pinched someone," she answered softly.

"I can't hear you, Kyari."

"I pinched someone."

"Pinched someone? We don't do that at the Rutherford School. Now take your tray and sit at that back table. I don't want to hear a peep out of you." I saw Kyari later in the day.

"So how did lunch detention go?"

"I was so scared of Mrs. Selkirk I didn't eat any of my lunch."

Kyari was stubborn and would get angry when other students ignored her or refused to be bossed around by her. A day or two later, she pinched another student. She was sent to my office.

"Kyari, you're not getting it. I'm putting you in lunch detention today in Mrs. Selkirk's."

"No, not Mrs. Selkirk's, anybody but her!" she said bursting into tears.

"It's not your choice young lady; this pinching has to stop."

So once again, down the hallway she went to Mrs. Selkirk's. This time she noticed how nice Mrs. Selkirk was to her fifth graders and was even allowed to interact with them. Mrs. Selkirk had one of her fifth graders read to Kyari. The situation kept evolving to the point where if Kyari behaved, she got to go to Mrs. Selkirk's class for a visit as a reward. A few days later, after more good reports from her teacher, Kyari popped her head into my office.

"Mr. Correa, I have something I want to ask you."

"Sure, Kyari."

"Do you think that when I become a fifth grader that Mrs. Selkirk could be my teacher?"

"Hmm, let me think about it, but it seems like you two would be a perfect match."

Fifth grade teacher and kindergartener had bonded. When they crossed paths in the office or playground, they would embrace in a heartfelt hug. When a student shows a willingness to turn around an unacceptable behavior, anything is possible and valuable life lessons can be learned. The key ingredient is the connection that develops between student and teacher.

No one told me that some kindergarteners are prone to wild out-of-control tantrums right in their classrooms. I hadn't seen this behavior with my own kids nor growing up in a big family either. I was taken aback by the severity of some of these episodes. It was only a few students, but the behavior was highly disruptive and labor-intensive as we attempted to get these kids under control. As is often the case, I was spending an inordinate amount of time dealing with a few regularly disruptive students.

In the office we began to use the funeral business term "removal." The secretary would inform me that I had a "removal" to do from one of the kindergarten classes. But unlike the undertaker, I didn't just load an inert body into a bag and throw it into the back of the hearse, I had to deal with a squirming, belligerent, out-of-control five-year-old. When I arrived on the scene, I would find desks and chairs overturned, books and crayons scattered about, and my little friend parked under a table refusing to come out. Often, teacher aides were standing around looking helpless as the teacher tried to continue her lesson. I would grab the student by the leg, drag them out from under the table, and swoop them into my arms, pinning their arms and legs so they couldn't kick, punch, or scratch me. I would then carry them screaming and wailing through the halls to the office and deposit them in the naughty chair until they calmed down.

The mayhem created in the classroom looked like a natural disaster had occurred: pages ripped out of books, crayons broken, tubs of supplies turned over, papers crumpled. Once our little demons (yes, they did seem possessed!), calmed down, they were sent back down to the classroom to clean up the mess they had made. These episodes could go on for fifteen to twenty minutes or even longer. Imagine as adults if we were having a really bad day at work and just collapsed to the floor, screaming and carrying on, throwing things, and ripping up reports. It might be delightfully cathartic, but we would be fired on the spot. They used to have primal scream therapy for people like this.

Kyle, who was as challenging a kindergartener as I ever met, was prone to wild and destructive tantrums. He was on the autism spectrum but on the Asperger's end, meaning he had normal language skills, and in his case, he was also very intelligent but lacked social skills. No matter what the diagnosis, poor Kyle had no impulse control and would blurt out constantly. He also had a bad case of work avoidance. His lack of social skills made making friends a virtual impossibility as he seemed to live in a self-centered bubble.   Empathy is a quality that we as educators are always trying to instill, cultivate, and recognize in students.  Sadly, Kyle had none.  He  couldn't connect with others and never remotely bonded with any of his teachers.  Kyle was a pudgy kid, too, so lifting and carrying him was a workout.   One time, I came into the room where he had been wreaking havoc.  He thought he would play a game and try to run away from me.  I used a simple but effective basketball move.  I faked one way and then pounced on him like a Bengal tiger, swooped him up, and carried him down the hall to the awaiting naughty chair.  I can still hear him screaming as we approached the office.

"No, not the naughty chair.  No, no."

Once, Kyle had an episode in the art room. It was my job as Assistant Principal to answer the call and remove him as he was disrupting the class by taking advantage of  an endless stockpile of art supplies to hurl at classmates and the art teacher. This was the last year of my career, but it seemed that I was going to go out with a flurry of kindergarten tantrums. I swooped Kyle up, and this time he felt heavier than ever, like a huge slab of feisty concrete. It was a long way from the art room to the office, and Kyle began to slowly slip from my grip until I finally managed to pin him on one  hip. I was sweating profusely as I wrestled my dead-weight cargo into the office and plunked him down on the naughty chair.  After dismissal, it was straight to the chiropractor for me. He noted that my hip was out of alignment half an inch.  Who would have thought after twenty-five years of teaching and administrating that I would be set out to pasture by a roly-poly five year old?

And then there was Keliyah, a cute little Latina who had long curly black hair and thick glasses that made her look like a research scientist or a brilliant intellectual.  Keliyah, in actuality, was the tantrum diva queen of the Rutherford Elementary School.

It was never clear if her tantrums were partially staged for effect.

She was a bit manic, so when she was on her game, she was a little too sweet and enthusiastic, but when she was off, it was catastrophic. It was difficult for her to strike any sort of balance and behave like a normal five-year-old.

Keliyah was a perfectionist and hated math. If she didn't understand right away, she had a fit. She would begin by throwing things: books, chairs, notebooks, scissors, basically anything she could get her hands on. And then, as if possessed by evil spirits, she would start telling her teacher how much she hated her, tell the other students to shutup, and then start screaming at the top of her lungs to her classmates "What are you looking at?"

When I was called down to remove her, Keliyah would start in with me. "Shut up, I hate you. You're ugly."

I would swoop her up and carry this bundle of fury down the hall. Sometimes, she would continue with her screaming and verbal abuse. At other times, she would ride along like a grand princess while I played, the courtier, assigned to carry royalty too disinclined to walk.

With Keliyah, it wasn't a simple matter of depositing her on the naughty chair. The one time we did that, she leapt off the chair, grabbed a yard stick, and took a swipe at our Principal, Mrs. Patterson, missing her head by inches. Her tantrums could go on for forty-five minutes to an hour. We would try putting her in the alternative learning center or barricading her in my office, but she would do her best to trash it. Finally, we decided the safest place to put her was the handicapped bathroom that also doubled as the men's bathroom. Well, she set right to work destroying it by breaking the soap dispenser, unraveling all the toilet paper including the unused rolls, and strewing the contents of the trash can all over the floor. This would continue until her mother arrived after we would call to tell her she had to take Keliyah home since she was too disruptive to stay in school. It was, in effect, an unofficial suspension.

In our meetings with her mother, we strongly suggested outside counseling, but mom was in denial, saying she never did this at home. We knew from talking to her cousins that Keliyah went off at family gatherings. Mom thought if she changed her diet, things would improve. Less sugar might help incrementally, but it wouldn't stop these outbursts.

The funny thing was that the other side of Keliyah's "Doctor Jeckyl and Mr. Hyde" behavior was that she could be utterly charming. I would be on "Keliyah watch" in the hallway in the mornings. Some days, she would come in with a big smile and come over to hug me. Other days, she had a menacing scowl on her face, a deeply furrowed brow, and an exhausted look like she hadn't gotten much sleep. One morning, Keliyah came up to me smiled, hugged me, and gave me a card she had made for me at home. I opened it up.

"Dear Mr. Correa,

Just you and me.

Love,

Keliyah"

So this was the flip side of the tantrums. In the end, Keliyah was a troubled little girl who needed help. We couldn't sit around waiting for her to outgrow these episodes. She was a danger to herself and others, and she was disrupting the learning process of other students. Eventually, as these tantrums continued into the first and second grades, she was placed in an alternative school until she was ready to return and behave according to the expectations that all the other students followed.

In dealing with these tantrums, I learned that the safety of classmates and the child were the first priority. Removing the-out-of-control student as quickly as possible minimized the chance that another student would be hit by a thrown object or that the troubled youngster would hurt herself. I had to remove the child and get her to a safe environment where we made it clear to the student that they would start over the next day with a clean slate. Some kids really needed counseling and outside support, so our clinical staff was closely involved in these cases. In school, we could not allow a student to disrupt instruction and prevent others from learning, yet at the same time, we were committed to working with each individual and trying to meet their needs while making sure the group didn't suffer as a result.

Most of all, I learned success with kindergarteners is mainly about relationship-building as it is with all kids. Talking to the kindergarteners when they're not in trouble, encouraging them, and hanging out with them in the cafeteria are simple ways to support them. Then, when trouble arises, they are much more likely to open up and trust that you will be there to help them through their problem or challenge.

In order to serve kindergarteners in ways that will cultivate their development, it's important to get a sense of how they tick. Talking to their teachers and parents and observing their classroom learning is essential.

And in the end, it is vital that we are open to what the kids can teach us. What right does a kindergartener have to demand that his Assistant Principal is out in the hallway every morning? So, when Patrick marched into the office and hounded me with "Mr. Caweer, Mr. Caweer, why aren't you out in the hall?" he was in effect acting as a spokesman for all kindergarteners by communicating in his unique way that they really liked being greeted and welcomed when they entered the building each morning. This was a great reminder that our clients or customers, who I was there to serve, wanted to be treated respectfully and with consideration - just the very thing we were asking of them in relating to their teachers and fellow students.

# Hoops

"Would you like to play basketball?" I asked Jamal, a troubled fifth-grader.

"Yes, Mr. Correa."

"I won't play with you unless you're getting the job done: treating your teacher right, getting all your work done, and getting along with the other kids, and no bus referrals. That's the deal."

"OK."

"I'm gonna want a week of perfect behavior. Think you can do it?"

"Yes sir."

"OK. Got another question. Who's gonna win when we play one-on-one?"

"I am."

"You are? You're making me laugh. I've never lost to a fifth-grader. I'm going to take you out there and give you an old-fashioned country whupping."

So began the male bonding ritual between one of the unruly students and his Assistant Principal at the Rutherford Elementary School in Monticello, NY. I can think of no greater counseling tool than basketball. So many of our boys came from households in which there was no father present, and they were not receiving the right kind of male guidance. It's the father's job, after all, to show his son how to be in the world. Boys that live with their mothers often times aren't respectful. They readily accept the doting, but mom isn't a scary physical presence. A father has a level of testosterone in his voice when he means business, and all young sons have a healthy fear of displeasing their fathers. I remember once telling my son when he was twelve or thirteen to get off the couch and start vacuuming the living room.  He gave me the "yeah, yeah, in a minute" until I raised my voice.  He was off the couch in an instant saying "alright , alright,"  and immediately began completing his assigned chore.

Since the gym was empty for the last half hour before dismissal, that was the time that I would have for these  one-on-one sessions during my thirteen year tenure as Assistant Principal from 2001-2014.   I kept a pair of black Nikes and a special leather ball in my office that I used only for indoor play.  Blazoned in big letters across it were the words "The Rock."  I was always on call in case a hoops session were to materialize.

The boys very quickly received a dose of hard-nosed reality.  They thought because I was an old man in their eyes (in my fifties) that they would easily blow by me and score at will.  I can still see their eyes expand like saucers when they instantly discovered  whatever move or fake they put on me was futile.  I was so much taller and faster.   With my wiry build, I could use my quickness to snuff them defensively by blocking their shots and stealing the ball at will.  Needless to say, my jump shot was unstoppable for a defender a foot shorter.  I told the boys I had played all my life and still played in a league that convened on Sunday mornings.  I was very much in touch with the game and still had hops.  It was important that they understood that I had worked a lifetime to develop my skills.

And I did deliver a "whupping," never letting up and usually winning by the score of eleven to one or two, even allowing the boys take the ball out after every basket.  It was an important lesson for them to see that in competition, no one was going to give them anything or take it easy on them.  After that, we got down to some more immediate learning.

"Jamal, do you want to be the starting point guard on the high school team?  It's going to take a lot of practice and dedication and love for the game.  Do you have that?"

"Yeah, my dream is to play in the NBA."

"First things first. You need to make the middle school team next year. Did you notice how easy it was for me to steal the ball from you? You just dangled it out there for me to pick you clean. Now watch me dribble. Notice how I keep my body between you and the ball. I'm protecting the ball, the point guard's most important job. No way you can steal it. Now you try it out, Jamal."

Jamal was a quick learner and picked things up in a matter of minutes. He had the ball so well protected I couldn't get close enough to steal it.

Next we moved on to shooting. Jamal was small, but as I told him, I was so tiny in fifth grade that I probably only came up to his shoulder.

"Jamal, why when you first came out were you hoisting up three pointers? You don't have the strength for that. It's nothing more than a heave. Get in the paint and practice layups and short shots where you can develop a rhythm. Bend your knees too. That will give you more oomph!"

We worked on that for a while.

"I'm making more of these than I usually do," Jamal noticed, a bit surprised.

"Well yeah, shooting is about squaring up and releasing the ball in rhythm. As you get bigger and stronger, you'll be able to shoot from further out and have a higher release point. When I first started playing as a second-grader, I shot underhand. I just didn't have the strength for an overhand shot. Over time, as I got taller and stronger, I was able to shoot overhand with a higher and higher release point until I had a fully correct release point above my head. But you have to know your range. I don't shoot threes. It's too far out for me, so my form falls apart, and my attempt becomes more of a throw than a shot."

Of course, I was just using basketball as a tool for creating a connection and building a relationship.  Some of our boys not only didn't have a father in their lives but never had male figures in their lives that hung out with them or spoke to them kindly.  It took a little while to see that what I was doing was really beyond "male bonding."  I was doing what I did for my own son and what all  competent fathers do:  showing our boys what it will take to survive in the world.

I reassured my student that despite our little "smack talk" previous to our game, I wouldn't tell any students what happened when they asked who won.  That would be up to the student to deliver the news and put whatever spin he wanted on it.  We would talk after playing, and often times the student would trust me enough to reveal something about himself.  Jamal did this time.

"I'm really angry with my father," he blurted out.  "I wish I could do stuff with him and talk to him everyday.  I don't understand all this adult stuff.  Why can't I live with him?"

"I don't know Jamal, but that's your situation.  This is the hand you were dealt, and you've got to play it.  Try to be aware of the anger and what you can do to keep it under control dealing with the teachers and situations with other kids here and in the projects."

Often times, for kids like Jamal, a relatively minor situation like a student cutting them in line, would blow up into a major incident as the smoldering anger rose to the surface and then blew up like a tornado.  There were successes and failures.  Jamal did go on to become starting point guard for the high school team.  I was most happy to hear that basketball motivated him to keep his grades up and that he would graduate on time.  I often attended Jamal's games.  He always made a point of coming over to the stands during warm-ups for a handshake and greeting.  I would always say, "Jamal, take care of the ball.  That's your job."  He would nod and look at me with a smile that said, "definitely heard that one before."

Another student that I worked closely with, David P., got in trouble frequently. He disrespected his teachers and got into fights. Once, in my office he told me, "I have a real anger problem."

The best advice that I could offer him was, "That's a good first step to recognize it. Now you're going to have to develop the tools to get it under control."

When he was an elementary student, I could see that David had the potential to be an excellent ballplayer. He did go on and made the varsity team as a sophomore in high school, but he never did get that anger under control. He joined a gang and got into criminal behavior. His gang leader ordered David and another member to beat up a guy who was messing with the gang leader's girlfriend. They not only put a severe beating on this guy, they also shot him to death. It took a year for the cops to get any witnesses to talk. David is currently serving a thirty-year jail sentence in the state penitentiary.

I was no doubt sad to hear all this, but I didn't feel like I failed. I know that when dealing with kids, no teacher or administrator saves anyone. At best we are an influence. Whether we influence the child then and there, or a year later, or further down the road, or never is out of our hands. Each person still has their personal fate or destiny to live out. One's influence may very well not be enough to overcome what's in store for that student. In addition, seeing yourself as a possible influence, rather than savior, lends an appropriate level of detachment to interacting with kids. Of course you love them, but they have responsibility for their own lives.

Once a student I will call Desmond was in my office. He wasn't in trouble, just visiting. He was a third-grader at the time, and I knew him as a needy kid who I made it my business to look after, especially since I knew his history. He was talking about how much he liked gym class when suddenly he started relating his traumatic incident from the past. He started telling me what happened and how he felt when his father shot his mother to death in their kitchen right in front of Desmond when he was four years old.   By the time he finished his story and we discussed it briefly, I needed a way to bring down the huge amount of emotional energy and grief that Desmond was expending.

"Desmond, how about we go the gym and shoot some baskets?"

We needed to do something physical that would balance both of us out after the heaviest discussion imaginable about the most gut-wrenching topic.  Once again, basketball to the rescue.  There was something so reassuring and therapeutically relieving about shooting some baskets and putting the heavy stuff aside.  Desmond was never good enough to play competitive basketball, but he loved the camaraderie and friendships he had made through the game.  He would return to his elementary school over the years to visit.  If I had the time, we would go into the gym and shoot baskets together and talk.  I could see how the court was a refuge for him.  He told me he had a great counselor at the high school and that he was more accepting than ever about his mother's death.  When he strode confidently across the stage to receive his high school diploma later that year, I was not only darn proud of Desmond but inspired by his journey and what he had overcome.

One year, we had a fifth-grade class that was just giving us fits.  There were a number of kids that were disrespectful to adults in the building and made lots of trouble in the cafeteria, on the playground, on the bus, and at their specials (gym, library, music, and art), in other words, whenever they left their teachers.  In the classroom, they generally could hold it together under the teachers' established routines, rules, and procedures.  There were ten boys that were what we call "at risk" students.  They were high maintenance and highly disruptive.  These kids were wreaking havoc in our school, so we needed some out-of-the-box strategy to rein them in.  Once again, we called on the great game of basketball to assist us.  With the aid of the Phys. Ed. teacher, Dave Holland, who volunteered his lunch period, we offered the boys a tightly structured basketball session three times a week during their lunch time in exchange for all-around improved behavior.  This included the ending of classroom outbursts, treating all adults in the building (including lunch aides) with respect,  getting their work done, and not getting any referrals.  The boys were all for it.  The moralists on the faculty complained that  only the squeaky wheels (the bad kids ) were getting the grease.  They wanted to see the rule abiding "good kids" get acknowledged for doing the right thing.

They also wanted any boy who messed up in any way, like not doing his homework, kicked out of the program.  We had to ignore this faction (thankfully we had the blessing of the principal), or we wouldn't have been able to offer this alternative.   It's always a mistake to pigeonhole students with the "bad kid" label.  It's vital to separate out the behavior and see the intrinsic "spark" that all kids possess.  View a child as a "bad kid" and don't be surprised if he fulfills that behavior.

And did the boys struggle with their new guidelines?  Of course they did.  We were looking for improvement.  If we made it tit for tat and a missed homework assignment meant no basketball, we would just end up with a disgruntled kid that we had set up for failure.   Better to be a little looser about it and let the kids make the connection between their behavior and the privilege we were presenting to them.  This seemed to work reasonably well.

With this group, there was no rolling a basketball out to them and letting them play a regular pickup game; they were way too out-of-control and uncooperative for that .  No, we spent the whole session on tightly structured drills to build discipline, dependence on each other, and camaraderie. We had them dribble around cones, do passing drills, and to test their commitment, engage in the one drill that is every basketball player's nightmare:  the dreaded "suicide drills" in which the players stand on the baseline and sprint to the other baseline touch the floor sprint back and continue back and forth until the coach mercifully blows the whistle.

We had mixed results of course. One boy, Gregory, missed a layup during a drill and stalked off the court.

"Gregory, don't worry, get back in there. No one makes them all," I urged. No, he made the choice to sit on the sidelines and pout. I wish I had been able to get him to understand that the best pros only make about 45 percent of their shots and that only through perseverance, hard work, and continual practice do you become a better shooter.

The boys progressed, but most importantly, the teachers saw improvement in their behavior. Probably the best thing we did for these boys was give them a reason for coming to school and something they could look forward to.

When you look at all the challenges that boys like these face, such as broken homes, abuse of all sorts, gang recruitment, neighborhood violence etc., school can be just a small part of their lives, or if they take advantage of it, a game changer and a way out of the poverty and the projects. They pretty much have to survive their upbringing in one piece to make it out.

Years later, some of the notorious ten came back to the Rutherford School to visit. It was downright inspiring to hear stories of college acceptances and big plans for the future. I also read in the paper about a few that we had worked so hard to guide onto the right road, who had still fallen by the wayside. One of our boys, Devante, used to rap at our assemblies and was already writing music as a fifth grader. Well, he threw away that marvelous potential and got involved with a group of kids that were robbing houses. They told the police when they were finally caught, "We're not a gang; we don't hurt nobody. We're a crew." In addition to stealing computers and other valuables, they stole a veteran's Purple

Heart. That didn't go over too big with Judge LaBuda, a military veteran, who sentenced them to ten years in the state prison.

One of the most difficult students to deal with is the unmotivated one. Most human beings are success-driven. If we're getting a lot of right answers in math class, it goes to reason we will like math. Carlos Martinez hadn't caught the success bug. He was capable but just wouldn't do any work. I nicknamed him "Señor Minimo." He did like basketball, and we had a private session, but even when I tried to set up hoops as a carrot, he wouldn't bite. He didn't take the invitation to play as any big deal. Meanwhile, it was a big deal for most kids to get an opportunity to go one-on-one against the Assistant Principal. There were plenty of kids begging me to play with them pretty much every day. For some students, whether it's basketball or some other activity, elementary school isn't quite the right time for something to click in their development.

I didn't see Carlos again until he was a senior at the high school. He came by to pick up his little sister. I barely recognized him after all those years.

"Got any plans for next year?" I asked him.

"Yeah, I'm going to college."

"Really, what do you want to study?" I inquired, now genuinely curious.

"Accounting."

"Accounting? Are you kidding? When you left us after fifth grade you didn't even know your times tables. What happened?"

"Well, something changed. In seventh grade I just decided I wanted to do my school work and get somewhere in life. It was my decision. I wasn't doing it for my parents. I found the motivation that I didn't have in elementary.  Now I wanted to do it for me."

Carlos always had the ability.  All it took was a shift in his attitude to start achieving.  Ironically, Carlos had reached the pinnacle of motivation.  It was now intrinsic and not dependent on outside rewards or incentives.  This young man was definitely on his way.

There was another type of basketball played at Rutherford, and that was recess hoops.  We had a spacious playground with three basketball courts.  The gung-ho boys wanted to play full court "street ball" which meant lots of ball hogging, dribbling with the head down, and general out-of-control play that was a trip to the nurse's office waiting to happen.  Since this kind of play involved a few kids tying up all the courts when we had over 150 kids on the playground at any given time, it wasn't efficient or practical.  This also prevented the girls from playing.  I explained to the boys that there are different kinds of basketball for different settings.  In your neighborhood, it can be street ball; in gym class, a skills-oriented variety; but recess with so many kids called for something else.  We figured out that a game called "Elimination" worked best.  Students would line up fairly close to the basket and take shots.  If you made it and the student behind you missed, they would be eliminated.

In the course of my rounds when I went outside to monitor recess, I would often join in or start a game of "Elimination" with students.  Unlike one-on-one, I stood a reasonable chance of losing if a student made a shot in front of me and I had to convert mine from a further distance.  Sometimes, I jokingly threatened students with a five day suspension if they had a shot to eliminate me.  It was good for them to see me joking about discipline.  They took great joy in sending me to the sidelines and were not shy about suggesting that perhaps I was the one who needed to serve a suspension.  Some of the shooting styles weren't pretty, but I saw students will the ball in, so intent were they on beating me and having bragging rights.  Of course after a little kidding and more suspension "threats," I would congratulate them for making the shots.

We felt fortunate at Rutherford that the great game of basketball was an integral part of our school makeup. We called upon it to be an exciting counseling tool, a means to relationship-building, a discipline alternative, and  a recess activity for fun and pure play.  Hoops is a all-purpose gem, a game that is not only a fun release of energy, but one that can play a meaningful role in a student's well-being and development.

# Summit Night

"I hate this.  Why did you make me come?"   Not exactly the words anyone wanted to hear as our climbing group was resting on a ledge at 17,500 feet above sea level on Mount Kilimanjaro at three o'clock in the morning on summit night.  My niece Kristine had directed these harsh words, tears of frustration welling up in her eyes, to her father- my brother, Bill.  It was tough going, and Kristine, like all of us, was suffering.  We all had more than enough on our individual plates just dealing with the lack of oxygen and had no energy or desire to get into any such discussion about the merits of the climb.  We were way past the point of no return.  I blocked out Kristine's assertion mainly because I just couldn't afford to go there.  I couldn't let my delicate confidence and will to summit be shaken in any way.  I guess I wasn't the only one feeling this way as all twelve climbers as well as the guides and porters, and especially Bill, remained silent.

It was our guide Dave Walsh who knew how to handle situations like this.  He was in his early sixties and had summitted Everest and the highest peaks on all seven continents.  He ran a technical climbing school in the highlands of Scotland.  He was a true mountaineering expert, of course, but his best attribute was reading people.  He spent plenty of time getting to know us before the climb to arm himself with knowledge that might come in handy when a climber was under duress, injured, or suffering from acute altitude sickness high up in the mountains.   It was Dave who broke the silence.

"Kristine, why don't I rope you to me, and we will go up together?" he said softly in a  firm yet soothing voice.  Kristine complied quietly like a school child being gently redirected by her teacher.  The next time I saw her, hours later, Kristine was happily planted on the summit a look of total elation on her face.

For many, climbing Kilimanjaro is an item on their bucket list waiting to be checked off. It wasn't for me. In the spring of 2006 I got a call out of the blue from my brother proposing that my fifteen-year-old son, Kevin, and I join him and his college-age twin daughters, Stephanie and Kristine, in climbing this major mountain on a faraway continent. I had three ready reasons for declining his offer: I had no experience in technical climbing, I didn't want to climb in snow, and I figured the expedition would be prohibitively expensive. I thought that was the end of it until Bill called me back about a week later and rattled off reasonable answers to all my objections. Kilimanjaro required no technical climbing: no ropes, no rock climbing, and no crampons. At worst it would be a grueling trek dealing with the 19,000-feet-plus altitude which, in its own right, was no small potatoes. We'd climb over the Christmas holidays during the dry season in Tanzania, avoiding any possibility of snowstorms on the upper reaches of the mountain. Surprisingly, the price of the airfares, the guide company, and equipment was much less than I originally anticipated. My objections now met, I asked Kevin if he was up for a challenging experience like this. He gave me a resounding yes, and now I was framing it as a family-bonding adventure.

Billy's inspiration for this venture was an article In the New York Times about a 65-year-old cancer survivor with one lung who opened his fortune cookie at his favorite Chinese restaurant and read the following: "As soon as you feel too old to do something, do it." He took that as the green light he had been waiting for to take up the challenge. He gave his best shot at climbing Kilimanjaro but his limited lung capacity forced him to turn back before reaching the summit. It was inspiring that he even attempted it.

So even though climbing Kilimanjaro is a fairly common bucket list item, it wasn't for any of us. We weren't interested in bragging rights or checking off some box like a list of chores to do around the house. What we did find appealing was that the climb would be epic in scope, there would be a challenging physical component, and that the outcome was by no means guaranteed.   We would get to push our limits and see the results.

I did my part to prepare for the climb by running up and down hills and going on long arduous hikes, but there is only so much you can do living at sea level in rural New York to prepare for the high altitude.  Still, it was important to have the hamstrings, quadriceps, and calf muscles in shape for the climb.  What turned out to be most important of all was acclimating properly.

Billy picked a guide company from England that had a high success rate in getting people to  the top.   Their secret was a well-thought-out and scientific program of acclimating.  The  most well-traveled route to the summit is called the Marunga Route, nicknamed the Coca Cola Route because it is supposedly the easiest ascension trail.   It also has the lowest summit success rate (near 60%) because people attempt to climb it unprepared and hire  the cheapest guides possible who are often unreputable and will rush people up the mountain.  This virtually guarantees altitude sickness and a quick aborting of the climb.

Our guide company, Jagged Edge, put us through a rigorous program to help prepare for the big climb.  Landing at Kilimanjaro International Airport after a grueling trip from halfway across the world, we made it to our hotel in Moshi late that night.  Next day, we were off to Arusha National Park to climb Mt. Meru, our warm-up mountain at 15,000 feet.

No one in our group had climbed to that altitude, but as it turned out this was the perfect way to acclimatize us.  We spent three days on this preparatory mountain that was a monster in its own right.  We got to experience a night climb to the summit that we would be repeating on "The Big K."  We also experienced the receding pinnacle in which we were fooled into believing time and time again that the summit was just over the next rise.  All of this was invaluable for the big climb to come.

After we finally reached the summit of Meru around sunrise, we returned to our previous hut and slept there that night. We were living the mountaineer's acclimatization adage to "climb high, sleep low" as the most effective way to prepare the body for the higher altitude. This allows for the greatest oxygenation of red blood cells. It is no surprise that it takes seventy days to climb Everest, such is the importance of this up-and-down acclimatization.

The following day we returned to our hotel in Moshi. Now, we were back down to 3,000 feet. The next day, we set off for our six-day expedition to mighty Mount Kilimanjaro, the peak looming just visible above the clouds at 19,340 feet.

The highest free-standing mountain in the world, Kilimanjaro is actually a volcano. It hasn't erupted in 360,000 years, so I guess it's safe to call it dormant. The mountain itself is divided into five climate zones: the cultivated lower slopes, the rain forest, the moorland, the alpine high desert, and the arctic zone. Much of the lower climbing, although steep, was quite pleasant as the temperature was comfortably warm and there were plenty of exotic plants and birds to observe. When we got to about 12,000 feet, it suddenly got cold as the temperature dipped and fog set in.

When we arrived at our final camp site at 15,740 feet, it was sleeting and frigid. As I lay in my sleeping bag pondering the ascent to the summit that would begin in a few hours, I was feeling much less gung-ho about willing myself to the top. The cumulative toll the climb had taken on my body and energy level was affecting my focus.

I thought about my students back at the Rutherford Elementary School. Our school motto was "Work hard and do your best because that's the Rutherford Way." So what was most important to model to my students? I believed it was either overcoming whatever challenges presented themselves or accepting my best effort whatever the result. It's one thing if best effort means overcoming discomfort and non life-threatening pain, but if certain altitude sickness symptoms manifest, it can be both foolhardy and dangerous to continue.

Still, I could feel the kids at school pulling for me, wanting me to succeed. Moreover, I really wanted to model what hard work, perseverance, proper preparation, and overcoming obstacles will get you. I had a banner that a teacher back at school had made for me to unfurl on the summit. It read, "Because that's the Rutherford Way." I envisioned an inspiring poster, our school banner proudly displayed on the top of Mount Kilimanjaro, that would hang on our school bulletin board for all the students to see as a reminder that they too could- and should-dream big. Mountain-climbing is a great metaphor as well as a concrete example of what we can accomplish when we set goals and then take the necessary steps to pursue our dreams.

I could hear Kevin and his cousins playing cards and laughing it up in the next tent over. It was clear that as far as family bonding, this trip was more about the cousins bonding. Kevin was such a natural climber that he moved up the mountain with relative ease. I was usually back in the pack plodding along. There was no need for any special bonding between me and Kevin. As a single dad, I was already very close to him.

I couldn't keep up with Kevin on either mountain because I was battling altitude sickness. Also the fact that I was 54 didn't help. This is a young person's pastime. Altitude sickness is caused by ascending faster than 1,500 feet per day (after reaching 8,000 feet) and exercising vigorously. No one, including individuals in super shape, is exempt from the fact that there is less oxygen in the air. On summit night, we ascended 3,600 feet from 15,740 to 19,340), more than double the ascent recommendation which just added to the inherent difficulties of high altitude climbing.

Altitude sickness, also called "acute mountain sickness," can manifest in a number of ways: headache, nausea, and extreme fatigue. These symptoms have to be monitored closely so they don't evolve into a possible life-threatening condition. H.A.P.E (high altitude pulmonary edema) causes excess fluid in the lungs, leaving a climber breathless even when resting. H.A.C.E. (high altitude cerebral edema) causes fluid on the brain. The only cure for the last two conditions is to immediately get the person down from the higher altitudes. Bill and I were tempted to take Diamox, a supposed altitude sickness preventative, but in the age of performance enhancing drugs, we thought that would taint our would-be accomplishment. Who wants, "yeah I summitted Kilimanjaro," but with an asterisk next to it?

I never did have headaches or extreme fatigue; instead, my altitude sickness manifested as stomach ailments on both mountains. It started as we headed down from Mount Meru. I felt nauseous as we began the final descent. Dave made me lead the whole climbing party despite the fact that I was moving at a snail's pace. He was afraid I would fall too far behind if I was in the back. "John, we don't want a pack of baboons carrying you off for dinner," he said half jokingly.

I just couldn't digest the greasy food the porters had been making for us during the climb. Usually it took forever for them to boil water at the high altitudes, so we ate dinner quite late.

Near the end of our descent from Meru, I spent time by the side of the trail in the rainforest vomiting. When I returned to school after the trip, a fourth-grader assured me, "You were just composting Mr. C." I was reminded of the time Mark Twain was seasick during a transatlantic voyage. A woman approached him and asked, "Mr. Twain, do you contribute to the Atlantic Monthly?"

"Hourly my dear, hourly," he responded.

Back in the oxygen-rich environment at the hotel, I felt better and dug into a dinner of eggy toast, French fries, and fried chicken. I ended up with the dry heaves back in my room.

No matter which mountain, I would often appear at our mess tent for dinner looking weak, pale and nauseous. I would eat only a few mouthfuls of rice, or plain toast and tea. I would quietly return to my tent and fall into a deep sleep. It was uncanny how many times I awoke the next morning bright-eyed, energetic, and ready to climb. Entering the tent for breakfast with a cheerful "good morning" seemed to surprise the rest of the climbing group. They began to call me "Lazarus." One of the great ironies of mountain-climbing is that the higher you go the less of an appetite you have despite the tremendous expenditure of energy and calories. I lost ten pounds on the climb and looked a bit emaciated at the end of the ordeal. Eventually, I figured out a way to eat that would work best for me. Instead of meals, I ate energy bars, taking a bite every twenty minutes when we were climbing. I combined this with Gatorade that I mixed from powder, making sure it wasn't too sweet so my stomach could tolerate it. This was like building a house for the first time: you learn many things along the way that you can apply to the next house you build. Unfortunately for many, there won't be another new house to apply all the lessons learned from the first one. And for me this, too, was a one-shot deal; there would not be another mountain.

After I lay in my sleeping bag wide awake for a few hours, we received the "wake up" call at 11:00 PM. It had come down to this: in about seven hours, if all went according to plan, we would be standing on the summit at Uhuru Point.

I had decided to store my hiking boots inside my sleeping bag to keep them nice and toasty as I attempted to sleep. This turned out to be a great move because even though we were only 240 miles south of the equator, we would face temperatures that night close to zero degrees Fahrenheit.

After a small bowl of oatmeal for "breakfast" at midnight we were finally ready to hit the trail at about 12:30 in the morning. It may seem crazy to climb at night. Surely it's much colder than during the day, but there are some very good reasons for it. High mountains often have their own weather patterns. On Kilimanjaro, clouds can easily shroud the summit by ten in the morning, obstructing the magnificent view of Mount Kenya to the north and Meru to the west. Also, the idea is not to dilly-dally around on the summit but to spend no more than an hour on the top and then make the descent to a safer altitude and more oxygen. And to go up from 15,000 feet to the summit in daylight would risk potential weather problems, a socked-in summit, and the risk of descending in darkness, which can be tricky.

As we set out that night, it was important to find a climbing rhythm. The steepness of the climb and the dwindling oxygen made this quite challenging. I kept my attention focused on the back of the foot of the climber right in front of me. The night lamps we all wore illuminated a small area just where the next step would go. The route that our guide company had chosen for us, the Umbwe, was the steepest, most difficult, and least traveled on the mountain. The guide company must have figured that we could handle a more arduous route after surviving their rigorous acclimation program. In any event, we saw very few fellow climbers even though we knew there were hundreds on the mountain.

As great a guide as Dave Walsh was, his knowledge of the local terrain was limited. For a night climb, we needed someone who could pretty much follow the trail with his eyes closed. Our local Tanzanian guide, Michael, fit the bill since he knew the nuances of all the routes. Dave deferred to his knowledge throughout the climb. After all, Michael had reached the summit over 250 times.

Another advantage to climbing at night was we couldn't see the precipitous drops or exposure right next to the trail. Having a fear of heights, I didn't need to be mesmerized and then potentially paralyzed and unable to move by a frightful drop next to the trail. My strategy, no matter what, was never to look down. Looking upward, I saw only the crystal-clear canopy of brilliant stars, a 360 degree view of each and every constellation imaginable.

When we did stop for breaks, it was impossible to get the heart rate down to resting pulse. Even taking baby-steps and moving as slowly as possible took extraordinary amounts of energy. It felt like I was in a continual state of trying to recover after running a hard and fast 400 meters. At sea level, you walk around for a while and eventually catch your breath. Up at 18,000 feet and beyond, there is no catching your breath. You breathe heavily, panting, your heart working overtime. This is pure physical stress that is very wearing and plays with your head.

It was vital as part of the preparation for the climb that I envisioned the end and saw myself on the top of the mountain. It was like when I play golf. I visualize the ball flight of a drive I am about to hit. It was important that my imagination give me a picture of what I expected to experience.

Finally at around 6:00 AM, we reached the rim. I was surprised to discover that the reality of the summit wasn't what I had pictured. I had imagined a gentle incline leading to the summit. The reality was quite different. The wind was blowing at gale force as we entered into the crater. A sandy, lunar-like landscape had to be traversed. We then approached a huge rectangular glacier at 18,500 feet. To the right appeared a severely-sloped rise, a miniature mountain in its own right. It was as if the summit were protecting itself, demanding one last proof that I belonged on the top. It surely felt like the "Final Test." I looked at this last stretch to the top, about 850 vertical feet and just succumbed to negativity and defeatism. I turned to my guide Dave and told him, "I can't make it."

In an exasperated and curt tone of voice he said, "OK, I'll get a porter to take you down around the glacier to a descent route. That's what you want?"

"No," I answered reflexively.

Dave knew exactly how to handle me. Now he was the teacher and I was the wayward student. I noted the irony as I recognized that Dave was using the same techniques that I used on students back at school. There are only so many approaches for getting a distressed student back on track. He had to challenge me on Mount Meru too, but here the whole climb was hanging in the balance.

At 19,000 feet, with only half the oxygen available at sea level, I was feeling the effects of this deprivation. I was disoriented and had trouble maintaining my balance. It was by no means life-threatening, and I could, if I were willing, overcome it and summit. I thought of my students and some of the challenges they faced: mom in jail for drugs, dad long-gone, food anxiety a daily concern, and the ever-present threat of gang activity in the public-housing-complex. And yet I would see kids dealing with these challenges by showing up at school everyday ready to learn. I was in awe of their upbeat attitudes. The tenets of our school motto, the Rutherford Way were, " attitude, responsibility, respect, teamwork, and fun." Now it was time for me to practice what I had preached. As is almost always the case in life, it's attitude that will carry the day.

Dave assigned a porter to carry my backpack. I was so grateful to receive this help. After we climbed switchback style across a steep sand dune-like incline, we entered a difficult rock section that demanded steady footing. The porter extended his hand to stabilize me through each and every difficult step. I was in awe of these beautiful Tanzanian souls that so reminded me of our support staff back at the Rutherford School. Both saw themselves as part of a dedicated team on a mission. The endurance they exhibited in carrying such heavy loads to support the climb was impressive, but it was their stellar attitudes that I admired the most.

As we continued to make our way through this final section, the porter now had me by the wrist and was literally yanking me to the summit. Now instead of baby steps, I was almost jogging and passing fellow climbers I hadn't seen all night.  They had astonished looks on their faces that said, "There goes Lazarus again!"  It felt as if my feet were off the ground and I was moving horizontally:  such was this magnetic-like pulling force from the porter.

Now everything suddenly flattened out and I could see the summit sign a hundred yards ahead.  I let go of the porter's hand and literally skipped that last little bit until I arrived at the highest point in Africa.  It was immensely satisfying to look out at the spectacular view and to know that the hard work and effort had been rewarded.

The story doesn't quite end there.  That morning after spending about an hour on the summit, we descended down a different route on the other side of the mountain and camped that night at 12,000 feet.  The next day we heard the news.  There had been a rockslide on the trail we had taken up the Western Breach to the summit, five or six hours after our group passed through.  Three climbers and at least five porters were killed.  We were the last ones to climb that section of the route before the rockslide.

A few days later while we were waiting for our flights at the airport, I talked to one of the survivors who had broken her leg in the rockslide. She told me that "When we woke up early that morning, we could see the lights from your head lamps  creeping up the mountain.  It looked like a procession."

I didn't have the heart to verbalize what was hanging in the air:  Yes, it was a procession all right, a funeral procession that we were in some eerie way foreshadowing.

# 5

# THE CHURCH AND MONASTERY

*I was brought up as a Catholic and went to church every week and took the sacraments.  It never really touched the core of my being.*

---Sting

### Survival In Service Of The Lord

Iron workers dangle from eight-inch-wide steel one hundred stories up.  Lumberjacks dodge falling Ponderosa Pines.  Soldiers disarm improvised explosive devices.  Movie stuntmen jump from burning cars at high speed.   Alaskan crab fisherman encounter fifteen-foot waves, gale-force winds, and frigid bone-chilling cold.  Surely these jobs at times can be life-threatening, but they pale in comparison to the dangers and mine fields an altar boy had to dodge in the Catholic Church in the 1960's.  As an altar boy I was dealing with uncomfortable pressure and anxiety.  There was the fear of messing up and being severely reprimanded if the duties weren't performed perfectly.  I never looked forward to serving Mass.  There was always the gnawing feeling that I would botch something in the upcoming service.  Much more importantly, I was spared from sexual abuse at a time when it was rampant in the Catholic Church.  That was a true blessing, and as more came to light about that dark age, it felt like a merciful miracle had been bestowed upon me.   Yet as big a deal as that was, I believe my greatest risk was that I would become a spiritual skeptic or even an atheist due to the lasting impressions and psychological scars I endured serving Mass as an altar boy under a tyrannical and insensitive parish priest.

I didn't volunteer to be an altar boy.  No one does unless they have a nascent vocation for the priesthood.  Like most others, I was forced into this thankless servitude by my parents, particularly my devout mother, at the Church of the Nativity in Fair Haven, New Jersey, where we were parishioners.  I knew at an early age that I just wasn't resonating with the whole Catholic trip:  the Mass, catechism classes, and the repetitive rituals.  It was going to take some sort of miraculous event or inspiring figure to bring me into the flock.  Perhaps a kind-hearted priest would demonstrate for me the goodness of the Roman Catholic Church...

Even at the age of ten, I struggled with the big picture inconsistencies. When it came to salvation, I could never understand what was to happen to the 1.2 billion living Chinese pagans, to say nothing of the billions that preceded them.  I guess they were just plum out of luck.  No Jesus Christ; hello limbo!  I was so tickled to discover years later that the "new" church theology eliminated limbo and made purgatory the all-purpose holding tank.

Our pastor, who as far as I knew never sexually abused any of his altar boys, was saddled with the sexually suggestive name of Father Hickey. He seemed to take delight in verbal abuse as he never could muster up the light touch of St. Francis, nor did his cheek ever seem to turn. Once, a woman, intent on receiving the Blessed Sacrament, innocently approached the communion rail dressed in her Sunday finest. God forbid, she was wearing her stylish gloves that were the signature touch to her outfit, matching her shoes and purse.  Father Hickey was not having it. "Take off the gloves," he sternly admonished with zero sensitivity to how devastating his words were to this sincere and devout Catholic.  Where was the loving redirection?  Father Hickey could have whispered a gentle word or two about next time or put an announcement in the church bulletin if this were so important. Instead, he just increased the sense of disconnect and killed any sense of spirit.  I felt so badly for this poor, pious lady .  And for God's sake, who wrote the rule, if there even was one, that women couldn't receive Holy Communion wearing gloves?

On one Christmas Eve, there was an unusually long line of both frequent and infrequent church-goers waiting to make their confessions. The posted schedule listed the time as 4:30 until 6:00. At 6:10 Father Hickey abruptly opened the door to the confessional and announced, "Confessions will end at 6:15. My dinner is getting cold."

Even as a young boy, I was incredulous. There were still a sizable number of people waiting, and some of them were the prodigal sons and daughters returning to the Church for their once-a-year confessions and Christmas Mass. Not the demographic that a parish priest should be further alienating. Was this a soldier of Christ working in the Lord's vineyard? It was appalling and diametrically opposed to the modeling of virtuous behavior that one would expect from their parish priest. I had serious doubts that I wanted to be a member of a church that allowed Father Hickey's repugnant behavior.

Before I even became an altar boy, I had already become a member of Father Hickey's select group of embarrassed parishioners. My brother Billy and I were late for Sunday Mass and decided to stand unobtrusively in the back. Father Hickey interrupted his sermon to let us know that this was somehow unacceptable. "There are plenty of seats in the front, boys."

He waited for us, with the eyes of the congregation upon us, to walk sheepishly down the center aisle and find seats before he continued with his sermon. Once again, I couldn't understand why Father Hickey was making such a scene. Did he really believe that public humiliation was going to make me a willing church-goer and a devoted parishioner?

There was no thought of insurrection. Father Hickey was our pastor, like it or not, and like most human beings, his behaviors spanned a range from the questionable to the admirable. His saving grace was that he gave short, digestible sermons that even a ten-year-old like me could track on. In addition, he possessed the driest sense of humor imaginable.

Once, my parents invited Father Hickey over for a drink. They welcomed him in at the front door, and my father took his coat as our pastor noted with no concern in his voice, "The child dangles from the roof." He was referring to one of my brothers who was playing around on a balcony outside one of the second story bathrooms.

Because Father Hickey conducted the affairs of the parish as if he were the C.E.O, he rarely called altar boy meetings. He delegated the supervision of the altar boys to an adult volunteer who handled the training and scheduling. The fact that he announced he would be attending one of our meetings raised our level of concern, as we knew he wouldn't be there to exchange pleasantries. Even a rookie like me knew our pastor would not be the bearer of good tidings. No surprise then when Father Hickey launched into a description of an incident the previous week in which one of the more veteran altar boys had almost set the altar on fire trying to light one of the tall candles that bookend the altar.

Father Hickey perched his cigarette in its holder precariously on the edge of the table as he explained the proper way to light the candles with the candle snuffer. On the back was a little knob that when slid forward would dispense a wick. If too much wick were pushed out, it would droop, causing an immediate fire hazard as well as making it impossible to light the candle. Father Hickey made it clear that only the older kids were to touch this troublesome candle snuffer. We were in teams. The older more experienced teenagers would serve with the ten to twelve year-olds to train them. I zoned out on the explanation, figuring it was the older kids' responsibility to deal with the candles.

Our demanding pastor wasn't done. "Gentlemen, the Latin is lacking," he flatly stated in that droll way of his. "There's too much mumbling."

We were always good for a few well-enunciated opening lines before fading off into muttering and incoherence. The Confiteor or confession was the signature Latin recitation prayer, and it came early in the Mass. Like most altar boys, I got off to a quick start with a solidly memorized first line, "Confiteor Deo omnipotenti, beatae Mariae semper Virgini." Perhaps Father Hickey was like the native speaker, hearing a foreigner who really can't speak the language, get off a good line and then assumes he or she can speak fluently. Unfortunately I took the Confiteor on a downward arc into a long string of mumbles followed by "mea culpa, mea culpa, mea maxima culpa" with a less-than-sincere, pretended-pious breast-beating with a closed fist. Then for the finale, a mumbling duet with my fellow altar boy in which the two voices merged on the wings of gibberish into one. Father Hickey wasn't buying it and told us to study.

He then reiterated our role to be unobtrusive as we supported whichever priest was saying Mass. He reminded us that our duties included preparing the altar, assisting at Communion, and supplying the priest with whatever he needed at the right moment. He was such a stickler for detail that he once complained that the water he symbolically turned into wine was lukewarm. He instructed us to run the tap longer until the water became colder. Must have been something in the divine symbolism I was missing...

Wouldn't you know it, I arrived to serve Mass the next week and the big kid, Perry, failed to show up. I had been at this only a few weeks and surely wasn't ready to serve solo. Daily mass is for the extremely devout, hardcore worshippers. As usual, it was exclusively older women in attendance: five or six octogenarians, rosary beads wrapped tightly around their fingers. With so few in attendance, the atmosphere was a bit more relaxed and less pressurized. The weekday Mass itself was much shorter without the sermon and long lines for communion. This was a relief as I thought there would be less chance for mishaps. Alas, that naive logic did not stand up to subsequent experience.

Midway through the Mass Father Hickey turned to me and whispered, "The candles aren't lit."

I left the altar and entered the sacristy in search of the candle snuffer. Perry had always taken care of lighting the candles, and now, I had to fulfill this challenging and dangerous task with no training. Now, I would pay for zoning out when Father Hickey was explaining it at the altar boy meeting. Suddenly, by default, I was the big kid and expected to know what I was doing.

I pushed that knob forward to expose a little bit of the wick and went to light it from a bank of prayer candles in an alcove on the far side of the altar. Then I returned to the altar and stood next to Father Hickey as he continued saying the mass. I looked up at the two candles looming high above the altar. I was a fourth-grader and tiny for my age. I might as well have been craning my neck to catch a glimpse of the top of the Empire State Building. Short of divine intervention, my task was physically impossible.

I turned to Father Hickey and said, "I can't reach the candles."

"Oh, why don't you just go away."

I returned to the sacristy devastated from this priestly putdown. I immediately began to weigh my options: I could return to the altar and clock Father Hickey with the candle snuffer, bolt for home, or go back out there and finish serving the mass. I chose the third option only because the first two would have meant major trouble at home.

After Mass, Father Hickey never consoled me, and of course, he didn't apologize for his mean remark. He could have made it a teachable moment and said something like, "Son, one of your responsibilities is to make sure the altar is ready for Mass. In the future always check to make sure the candles are lit. If they aren't, let me know." Any Christ-like compassion was nowhere to be seen. Instead I found myself continuing to disconnect from a Catholic Church whose worldly representative apparently had no heart and preferred to scold rather than to mentor.

As time went on, I became the "big kid" and my younger brother Billy the apprentice. We started with a weekday 7:00 AM Mass. We were never crazy about getting up at the crack of dawn. We lay in our beds and prayed as fervently as we could that devout Mom would forget or oversleep. Our prayers went unanswered as she never did, not once.

After a while, Billy became more comfortable with the routines and procedures. We finally got the call for the big show, Sunday Mass! This felt like the leap from rehearsing a play to opening night with a huge audience in attendance. Everything was magnified under the bright lights, including any mistakes we made. Billy was a charming little boy with an engaging smile, but he could be a bit dreamy if not an all-out space cadet. Once, he wasn't watching where he was going and tripped on the hand bell. This would not have been a big deal at weekday Mass, but it was disruptive under Sunday's scrutiny, creating a discordant racquet and a stare-down from Father Hickey.

On another occasion, Father Hickey gave the hand signal for us to switch the Epistle book and a cloth called the altar protector from one side of the altar to the other. Billy was apparently day dreaming and didn't see the signal. Father Hickey gave the signal again and still no response. This was like a baseball manager coming out to the mound to replace his starting pitcher, signaling to the bullpen by gesturing with his arm that he wanted the lefty, and nobody out there was watching the proceedings on the field. Finally on the third attempt, Father Hickey turned around and addressed Billy quite sternly, "Will you move the Book?"

One Sunday, Billy and I were preparing for the "washing of the hands," a ritual in which the priest symbolically prepares for the consecration and the reception of the Holy Eucharist. Over at a side table, I picked up a small cruet filled with water and draped a thin white towel over my left forearm. Billy picked up the container to catch the water that I was about to pour over Father Hickey's hands. I would pour and Billy would catch the water as it fell through our pastor's fingers. While not as complicated as a trapeze act, timing was of the essence. When Father Hickey extended his fingers, I poured. For whatever reason, Billy spaced out again and did not extend the container to catch the water. Father Hickey peered over his reading glasses perched on his nose and observed dryly, "You know boys, that water just went into my shoe."

Our response was to look down and carry on with the job however incompetent he thought we were. Now, we focused on trying not to mess up rather than on serving the Lord. Thanks to Father Hickey, serving Mass had become even more of a grim, nerve-wracking chore.

As it turns out, these altar boy traumas tend to span the generations. My father, who grew up in Brooklyn, New York, told the story of his nemesis, Father Jacob, or Father Jake as he was known by the community. Father Jake was the Principal of Brooklyn Prep High School. One early September day in 1927 when Dad was a freshman, my grandfather arrived at school to take his son out of school early to get to Yankee Stadium in time to watch Babe Ruth play. My grandfather was fanatical about baseball and still played hardball into his 50's. He would gather every Wednesday afternoon to play baseball with his doctor friends who were off for the afternoon. They hired umpires and played on a manicured diamond they rented from a local semi-pro team, fantasizing like young boys, they would one day hit a majestic home run like the Babe. Now, Grandpa had to convince the Principal that a trip to Yankee Stadium would be an educational "field trip." Well, Father Jake wasn't having it. He would not release Dad from school. Grandfather and Principal engaged in a heated discussion. Father Jake evidently had no respect for the Babe.

"He's an overweight philanderer who is not only a glutton but a big drinker and carouser. What kind of example is he for our young men?"

Of course, Father Jake was oblivious to Babe Ruth's prodigious ability to hit the long ball  and how in 1927 by belting sixty home runs, he was revolutionizing baseball.  Against Father Jake's will, father and son departed for Yankee Stadium.  Dad knew he would pay for this.  The next morning he was called to the office where Father Jake awaited.

"You will be spending the next two weeks in jug." ("Jug" is an old fashioned word for after-school detention.)

A few months later, Dad was serving at a funeral mass at which Father Jake was the presiding priest.  Suddenly, Father Jake bull-rushed my father, frantically grabbing him and trying to throw him to the floor.  Dad figured his Principal had just flipped out, probably deciding to  punish him some more for the Babe Ruth incident. His Catholic guilt told him he probably did deserve more.   No, as it turned out, Dad had backed into a bank of funeral candles during the procession and the back of his cassock had caught on fire.  Father Jake was doing everything he could to save his young soul.

For my Dad, being an altar boy literally did, for a few terrifying moments, become the most dangerous job in America, as it obviously did for any boy who was sexually abused in that sinister era in the 1960's.  I was able to survive my encounters with Father Hickey, my psyche still intact, but I was done with the Catholic Church.  The danger I skirted was that the Catholic trip could have been a "one and done" experience, leaving me embittered, skeptical, and cynical toward all spiritual endeavors.  It actually had the opposite effect. Because my altar boy experience was so demoralizing and distasteful, I was inspired to become a seeker.   Father Hickey not only provided a test to see if I could survive his cruelty, but he also did me a favor by helping make it crystal clear at an early age that I was not to be a Catholic.

I hoped that I would find something that would provide a deeper meaning and purpose to life which, after my traumatic altar boy experience, would be a welcome step up.   Whatever my high-water mark turned out to be, I was hoping that I would eventually resonate with something. How much worse could it get? There had to be something better out there.

In some ways, a spiritual search is like looking for the right vocation. You try out a few different occupations until you find one that fits. Maybe working in an office for the company hierarchy isn't fulfilling, but working with kids is. After a process of elimination, one hopes to find the right niche.

I eventually did find something that provided me with the meaning I was looking for. After looking under quite a few rocks, I was drawn to an individual, interior path in which help is provided through a daily practice.

Now, many decades later, as I look back at my experiences with Father Hickey, I can see that this dour parish priest unconsciously prodded me, an impressionable ten-year-old boy, to dig deeper. It's as if he were put there to make sure I had a negative experience in the short term to lead to a greater one later. So even though serving Mass was an anxious and joyless exercise in fear of failure, my experience with Father Hickey was a stepping stone. So in the end, I am grateful to you, Father Hickey. Thank you, thank you so very much!

# The Trappist Retreat

By my early forties, I had acquired the outer signs of success and happiness: a wife and nuclear family with the requisite 2.2 children, a satisfying job , a nice house, and enough money to live comfortably, yet nagging doubt persisted. Was there more, a higher purpose? I was still a seeker for truth and a more profound take on the meaning of life. The big three nagging questions still remained: "Who am I? Why am I here? What is the means of transcendence out of this sorry world of cause and effect, duality, and the prison of the mind/ego?"

I also wondered if there was a more harmonious way to live. The hustle and bustle of modern living left very little time for reflection and contemplation. The rat race left me with the feeling that life was passing me by without making enough sense of it...

I was raised Catholic but could never resonate or feel any inner connection to the rituals. The fact that the Church was imposed on me and that I never chose it was also a factor in my disenchantment. However, I was intrigued by and admired the Cistericians, better known as the Trappist Monks. It was Thomas Merton who brought attention to the order and the monastic life with his best-selling autobiography in the 1950's entitled *The Seven Story Mountain*. Not only is the book spiritually inspirational, Merton also chronicled his life before he became a monk, recounting incidents of drinking and encounters with the opposite sex. The church tried to censor his book, but enough of Merton's experiences came through for me to see that Thomas was a normal red-blooded, young-male before he committed himself to the monastic life.

I discovered that the Trappists allowed visitors to their monasteries. The nearest one was Our Lady of the Genesee Abbey in Piffard, New York, about an hour outside Rochester and about a four-hour drive from where I lived in Pennsylvania. I arranged for a weekend retreat, anticipating that I would learn something from these contemplatives that had renounced the world.

Upon arriving at the monastery's bucolic setting in the quiet secluded countryside, I quickly settled in my guest room and then sat down for the suggested interview with Brother David, the monk in charge of the retreat house and the orientation of the visitors.

"So John, how long have you felt called to committing your life to spirit?" asked Brother David quite directly.

"I never have. I hate the Catholic Church."

Brother David laughed good naturedly then followed up with the next logical question. "So, why are you here?"

"I don't know why exactly. I guess I want to check out what the monks are doing, observe how they live, and see if there's anything I can learn from them."

"Fine John. Plenty of our visitors have a deep curiosity. I believe there is a part of all of us that calls us to a higher purpose in life. Some resonate with that feeling; others ignore it. Just be open to what you experience this weekend."

My first decision was to choose whether I wanted to eat my meals in silence or be free to talk to the other visitors. I opted for the latter as I was also interested in hearing what had drawn the others to make this retreat. For some, it was getting away from their busy lives and taking stock; for others, some serious interest in becoming a monk. In either case, they tended to be over-the-top Catholics: the type that would attend weekday Mass religiously and carry rosary beads in their front pocket. They were a bit too "Catholic" for me to engage any of them in an open conversation about spirituality.

The monks have dedicated themselves to a life of labor, Lecto Divina (divine reading), and prayer. They must also be self-sufficient, their labor producing something that will support them. At the Genesee Abbey, the monks make a tasty bread that they sell at their bakery and to stores around the Rochester area under their simple label, "Monks Bread."

The Trappist tradition of quality products is world-wide.  The Belgian monks make their famous beer with a secret recipe that contains residual sugars and living yeast, that unlike conventional beers will improve with age like fine wine. Other products sold throughout the Trappist world include cheese, fruitcake, clothing, and even coffins. There is something reassuring in knowing that when you are lowered into the earth to rest in peace for eternity,  the fine quality of the box you find yourself in was meticulously crafted by the Trappists!

Yet, it was because of this superior quality and the monks' attention to detail that they became victims of their own success.  The Monks Bread was so good that naturally the demand for it increased.  The contemplatives' mom and pop operation started to feel pressure from the outer capitalistic system to expand.   The Monks now had to deal with the problem that the profits were more than they needed to sustain their lifestyle.  As modern life quickened with Internet sales, the monks have adapted.  They have tried to protect their lifestyle by farming out some of their production.  They even sold the bread recipe to a huge regional bakery in Florida.  The monks go corporate!

The daily schedule of the Trappist is far more severe than any marine boot camp.  At Genesse the rigorous routine is exacerbated by the fact that they are bakers.  Communal prayer in the dead of night and baking long before the sun rises are uneasy companions, especially for anyone that values sleep. The daily schedule is as follows:

2:10:  rise

2:25:  vigils,* breakfast, lectio (divine reading)

6:00:  lauds,* mass, thanksgiving

7:00:  terce,* work

10:30:  end of work, lectio

11:15:  sext,* dinner, optional siesta

1:10:  end of siesta, work

3:30:  end of work, lectio

4:30:  vespers,* supper, lectio

6:35:  compline*

7:00:  retire
    *common prayer

Yikes! The monks were ruled by the clock like factory workers on the assembly line. Like summer camp for wayward children, every moment was accounted for. Perhaps a bit of concern that the idle mind is the devil's workshop?

The monks gather seven times daily for communal prayer. Of course, the visitors were not expected to keep up with this schedule, but I did get up the first night to make vigils in the chapel. It was a violent awakening to get up at 2:00 A.M. Somehow, I managed it and stumbled out of the guest house. The walk to the chapel was about half a mile, a full moon guiding the way, the beacon of the lit-up chapel off in the distance. The wheat the monks grow for the bread was waving in the delightful summer breeze directing me to the chapel. As I approached, I could hear the faint intoxicating sound of Gregorian Chant. What is it about the sublime harmonies of this sacred music that just opens us up to something deeper within? The monks lead a hard life, but it is through this mesmerizing and tranquilizing singing that they manifest their joy and love of the Divine and express their devotion to God. After about an hour of this prayer service, I headed back to the guest house and went right back to sleep. I had to be up again for six o'clock Mass. By the time I ate breakfast at 7:15, it felt like it was about four o'clock in the afternoon.

As I walked around the property during the day, I would occasionally see a monk fly by on a tractor.  With all the work growing and harvesting the wheat, as well as the relentless baking operation, there wasn't a moment to waste, especially with all those communal prayer services to attend during their waking hours.  Watching these "mad monks" driving around at 35-40 miles an hour, it became obvious that they must have souped up the engines.  This mad dash existence didn't strike me as particularly contemplative.

We also envision monastic life as very quiet and peaceful, and it is for the most part at the Genesee Abbey.  The bakery is the one exception. As the operation increased in size, more automated machines were brought in.  Many of them, like the automatic bread slicer, cause quite a racquet.  Even with ear plugs, it was difficult to reflect on the latest lectio divina or hear yourself think for that matter.  Kind of puts a damper on the monastic tradition when the clanking machines at  the work site sound like a pneumatic drill.

The highlight of the weekend was meeting and getting to talk to Brother Gregory.  His official title was porter or, literally from Latin, the keeper of the gate.  He was in his eighties and had plenty of stories to tell about  the life of the Trappists  back in the day.

"We were under news blackouts:   no newspapers, magazines, nor radios.  One day in the summer of 1945 our Abbot, Brother Michael, gathered us together and announced, 'Gentlemen, there has been a world war.  It's over now.  We won.' That was it.  No details.  It was years before we knew the particulars."

Once Brother Gregory caught a glance of a Life Magazine that was sitting on the front seat of a workman's truck in the 1950's.  "Yeah, there was a young guy on the cover.  I don't know what he did, but his name was Priestly I think, but I'm not sure."

It took me a few seconds, but I finally blurted out, "Do you mean

Presley? Elvis Presley?"

"Yes, that's him. What did he do?"

"He was a famous singer."

I didn't have the heart to tell this cloistered monk that Elvis was a significant influence in loosening up America's puritanical sexual mores.

Back in those days, speech was seen as a negative disturbance to a monk's quietude and receptivity, possibly even tempting a brother to exercise his own will instead of the will of God.

"We didn't speak during the week, but we were allowed to converse in Latin on Sundays. And it wasn't like we didn't communicate. We had an elaborate sign language that covered just about everything we needed to say."

Sounds like a maximum security prison in some ways. Visits, including family, were confined to one weekend a year. The idea was to completely let go of the outside world.

The weekend I was there happened to fall on a Saint's feast day, so a con-celebrated mass in which more than one priest participated was planned as some of the monks were also priests. Brother Gregory asked me if I would participate in the Mass by performing the simple task of bringing the unconsecrated hosts up to the altar when he gave me the signal. And I thought I had bid a good riddance farewell to my altar-boy days. Well, I suppose it wouldn't hurt to come out of retirement for one final encore, would it?

When the moment of truth came, I had already lost my focus, carried away by the soothing, and hypnotizing Gregorian Chant that the monks sang so beautifully. Suddenly I felt beads of perspiration forming on my forehead. Something wasn't right. I began to flash back to traumatic altar boy experiences from my distant past. Then as I snapped out of my disturbing terror, I noticed out of the corner of my eye Brother Gregory gesturing like a madman for me to bring the hosts up to the altar. Remember this was a man who could speak fluently with his hands...

When the weekend ended and I was able to reflect on my impressions of these noble contemplatives, I felt both a tremendous admiration for their devotion and a bit of disappointment that they adhered to such a strictly mandated schedule. Not a lot of free time for needed solitude. It's no wonder they had to race around in souped-up tractors or risk being late for yet another session of communal prayer.

The monks committed themselves to a life of common and private prayer, sacred reading and study, manual labor, service to their fellow monks, and hospitality to a curious public. It's a tall order to fulfill all these commitments. Not only is making a living very time consuming, but apparently communal prayer takes precedence over private prayer. Isn't silence the gateway through which the devotee enters contemplation? There's a built-in paradox to being a community of hermits.

The monastic life has been described as sometimes Eden and sometimes a battleground. Petty feuds and exaggerated personality conflicts all come with the territory of the well- intentioned moral attempts to subdue the mind. As the demons arise, they are often projected onto others. Yes, even monks deal with the shadow.

Yet as tough as that is, renunciation is the real killer. Does giving up smoking or drinking makes you a better person? No, you only become a non-smoker or a non-drinker. So by leaving the world, by renouncing it, does that make the monks any more spiritual than the rest of us? I think not. We know intuitively that we can carve out a spiritual life in whatever situation or circumstances we find ourselves in. I wonder if by removing themselves from the world, that the monks may find their growth stunted by not facing the challenges of relationships, family, job etc. that the rest of us encounter. Are the monks trying to conveniently escape their karmas by leaving the world behind?

The mind can easily fixate over something it has been denied. Years ago, I was attending a relative's wedding. Due to their religious customs, the groom's parents asked that there be no dancing or alcohol at the reception. It was a scorching hot afternoon in July on the East Coast. The no alcohol request made beer a "forbidden fruit" to the many Irish–Americans in attendance. We became obsessed with the thought of imbibing an ice-cold, thirst-quenching beer. It was all most of us could think about. After the formal reception, we went back to the hotel and, joined by the bride and groom, had the "real reception" with plenty of fine beers purchased at the corner liquor store. When we discovered that we didn't have an opener, one of the brothers-in-law volunteered a solution and began to open the bottles with his teeth. This is the nature of the mind when it feels denied. It probably was the best, most satisfying beer of my life. I wonder if the Belgian Trappists after a long day of brewing, ever kick back, pour themselves a tall brewsky, and contemplate the Lord.

The Rule of Saint Benedict which govern monastic life states that the monks' life should be centered upon common prayer, meditative reading, and manual work. I wonder if this is a bit too compartmentalized and restrictive for a balanced life. There's no mention of play.

Wouldn't it be healthy for monks to throw a Frisbee around, go bird watching, or even play golf? I would love to see a monk's response after missing a three foot putt! We can learn just as much from our avocations as our vocations. We know from life on the outside that play is our balance to work. At school, we have recess. Perhaps the monks, just like kids, need to get out in the fresh air and play on the jungle gym. They could even trade in one of their common prayer times for monastery recess and take a play break. If they needed to multi-task, they could sing Gregorian Chant while playing dodge ball...

# 6

# THE DEARLY DEPARTED

*Die happily and look forward to taking up a new and better form. Like the sun, only when you set in the west can you rise in the east.*

---Rumi

### Six Feet Over

I once lived with my teenage son, Kevin, in an apartment above a funeral home in the tiny hamlet of Callicoon, New York. Most people thought our living arrangement was somewhat unusual or just plain weird. They probably imagined spirits of the dead wandering around the premises or, if not that, death was something they would prefer to keep at a much greater distance.

Of course it was circumstances, not some casual decision or macabre fascination with death, that resulted in my decision to sign the lease and move in. Kim Murphy, a fellow teacher at my elementary school in Monticello, New York, lived above the funeral home with her husband Mark, the funeral director, and their two daughters. They were about to move into a new home and suggested that Kevin and I move into the apartment. Not only would my commute to work be cut in half, but their daughter Lindsey and Kevin were the same age. She quickly introduced Kevin to the other kids at school and he instantly made friends. Initially Kevin had resisted the move, but it didn't long for him to appreciate that he was in a much better situation.

Daily living at the funeral home was generally low key. Wakes and funerals were fairly infrequent. When we first moved in, there were approximately eighty services a year. By the time we moved out eleven years later there were only about fifty, due probably to the changing snowbird demographics. The funeral director still half-jokingly blamed us for the drop off, but it was hard to feel guilty about fewer people dying...

We enjoyed the benefits of funeral home living. Unless there was a viewing, it was quiet, pin drop quiet, a perfect backdrop for undisturbed reflection. In addition, we were never concerned about locking our doors. Who's going to break into a funeral home?

Halloween passed quietly with no fuss whatsoever. Not only were Mischief Night delinquents too spooked to come near the place, I never made any effort to stock up on candy. The kids were too afraid to knock on the door as they were half expecting a corpse to sit up from a coffin and scare the living daylights out of them.

My landlord Mark, and his twin brother, Matt, ran the Stewart-Murphy funeral homes in both Callicoon and nearby Jeffersonville. Since Callicoon had the embalming facility, all bodies came to Callicoon first no matter where the  wake or funeral took place. As Mark was fond of saying, "The road to heaven goes through Callicoon."

In the funeral business, retrieving the corpse from a rest home, morgue, or residence after the death certificate has been signed is called a removal. A body would arrive anytime of the day or night. Since my bedroom was above the garage, I was always awakened by the middle-of-the-night arrivals. I would be jolted out of deep REM sleep by the sudden engagement of the garage door opener. As the droning guttural sound of the hydraulic gurney suddenly became activated, I would pass through a brief period of disorientation before realizing where I was and that yet another fresh corpse was descending  into the bowels of the building on its way to the embalming chamber. Now wide awake and back in my body, I would lie there under the covers imagining how this particular incarnation ended. Was it peaceful? The whole family gathered around as grandma slipped off into eternity, a beatific smile on her face. Or was it a sudden heart attack? Or did the deceased fight a disease and then struggle to let go? In any event, I would get the lowdown the next day when I spoke with the funeral director.

The longer I lived above the funeral home the more accepting I became of this new normalcy. At the same time, I wanted to know more about what transpired downstairs in the mortician's laboratory. I asked if I could witness an embalming procedure, but was told only licensed undertakers could be present. It made sense that the public was excluded with the potential for legal issues and the shock they might experience seeing their loved ones in that lifeless state. It's probably best for everyone that the world's ultimate makeup artists labor in solitude...

As I watched yet another casket being loaded into the hearse, the sobering reminder to live with a sense of urgency was poignantly apparent. Make hay while the sun shines; do whatever is necessary to embrace the path of increased awareness. One seeming paradox is to learn how to die daily. As we live our lives, we can, if we choose, freely die to worn out, counter-productive attitudes and points of view that no longer serve us.

The obituaries were required reading. I poured over the Times Herald each day to try to keep abreast of the visitation hours in case I didn't see Mr. Murphy. More importantly, I wanted to know a little something about the life journey of my fellow tenant during his brief stay downstairs.

At times when I parked my car in the garage, I still had no idea if there were viewing hours that night. I would walk up the ramp leading to the funeral parlor and to my apartment upstairs. Sometimes the door was wide open. I would see an open casket with the deceased prepared and ready for that night's viewing, surrounded by huge bouquets of lilies, carnations, roses, and other appropriate funeral flowers. I always found lilies, as a symbol of innocence restored to the soul of the departed, to be a touching and poignant reminder of our sublime journey back Home. Initially, I was startled to see a corpse suddenly come into view, but in time it became quite ordinary. I would walk into the parlor and approach the casket to take a close look and visit a bit, just the two of us. After a little commiserating about where we had been and some conjecture about where we were going, I would bid the departed soul a sincere goodbye and wish it well on the next stage of its journey.

As competent as the twins were at the embalming process, I could never get over how fake and rubbery the skin of the deceased looked. Thanks to the mix of formaldehyde and other chemicals, the body was made to look "presentable" for the viewing. The age-old observation at the wake "Doesn't so and so look good?" is a real stretch. The life force is gone, and only an empty carcass remains.

Once when I was quietly heading up the stairs to my apartment during a service, I overheard a young minister struggling to make this spiritual point in a eulogy. He evidently gestured to the open casket and said, "The body of our beloved friend Larry is but a shell and the nut is gone..."

No doubt this living arrangement has changed my relationship with death. My level of concern has been raised by the relentless reminders of "for whom the bell tolls." Even when the funeral home was deserted, I could still hear the somber, haunting sound of the dirge resonating throughout the building. If not that, then the startling sound of the buzzer downstairs alerting me that I needed to open the garage door. The delivery man from the Bates Casket Company was there to drop off yet a few more coffins in this endless procession of arrival and departure. Seems like there has to be more to it than doing your seventy dutiful years and then being shipped off, if you can afford it, in an ornate mahogany box.

One of the great mysteries of life is to live out our individual sojourns without specific guidelines. Much of what we do depends upon what we are drawn to and what captures our attention and devotion. It may be serving others, loving our partners and families, or pursuing outer ambitions.  We can all do these things but still feel unfulfilled and that something is missing.  Some of us may become seekers on the age-old quest to find deeper meaning in life. Living above the funeral home seemed to crystallize three questions for me:  Who am I?  Why am I here?  What is the means of transcendence?  The answers, I believe, lie in one's readiness to embark on the interior journey.

During a wake, there was often a perceptible hum we could hear arising from below.  It sounded as if people were enjoying themselves at a cocktail party, catching up on the latest with old friends and dropping any lugubrious behavior they may have adopted for the occasion.  This was especially true when the deceased was someone very old who had lived an honorable life.  The service was more celebration than mourning.  What was much tougher to reconcile, of course, were younger people dying from diseases, drug overdoses, or car accidents.

Kevin in his bedroom was also subjected to the disturbing late night racket of the hydraulic lowering dead bodies to the embalming facility.  He told me that his first thought was always to pray that it wasn't someone he knew.  But, of course, on occasion we knew the deceased and would solemnly walk down the stairs to pay our respects just like any other mourners.

One day Kevin came home from school upset, his eyes red from crying. A classmate was killed by a drunk driver as he was walking home along route 97.   My son not only had to sit next to the empty desk in school but then come home knowing his friend's remains were in the mortuary downstairs.  Now death was no longer abstract.  It was immediate, and Kevin was grieving again.

Two years before we moved in, Kevin's mother was killed in a car accident.  I thought that living above the funeral home  would help ameliorate Kevin's grief as he experienced the normalcy of death as part of life. I had hoped this would better help him come to terms with his great loss. Over the years, I was moved to see Kevin willingly counsel peers who had lost loved ones.

On one occasion we were downstairs at the wake of a school acquaintance who died of an overdose. Kevin was an anchor of support for the kids who were busted up by the sudden passing of their friend. He was consoling the bereaved and helping them come to see that they were not alone. I couldn't make out his exact words but could sense his gentle and tender tone. A gangly six-foot-three, Kevin draped his long arms around his friends and gave them hugs that were both heartfelt and soothing. These interactions were so intensely private that I never brought them up or discussed them with Kevin. I just marvelled at his compassion and maturity.

In this funeral home atmosphere, I often reflected on my own personal situation. It felt as if Kevin's mother, Colleen, had died twice: once when our marriage dissolved and again when she was so suddenly taken. Honestly, her first "death" was more painful to me than her actual final exit.

I must say that on the mundane level, it was actually quite easy to live above the funeral home. There were not a lot of requirements or rules we had to follow. During a wake or funeral, I had to move my car out of the garage to provide access for the hearse. Otherwise, it was pretty much about being quiet. No running of the washer or dryer, no loud music, and no sudden, disturbing noises.

One Sunday afternoon, Kevin and I were watching a football game while a funeral was taking place downstairs. A Dr. Jekyll/ Mr. Hyde transformation overtakes me when I watch my favorite team, the New York Giants. I was no longer comporting myself as I did in my day job as the mild-mannered assistant principal, mediating disputes , placating teachers, and attempting to model good citizenship. Kevin and I were rabid fans. As the Giant faithful, we were, nevertheless, fatalists who considered the two recent Super Bowl wins as generous and miraculous gifts from the football gods. In most years, we expected things to go wrong, and they usually did. We were not above yelling or criticizing the players on our flat-screen TV as if they could hear us. There was Eli Manning driving our beloved Giants to what we hoped would be the winning touchdown late in the fourth quarter against the despised Dallas Cowboys. Eli dropped back to pass and had a receiver wide open in the end zone. Inexplicably, he threw the ball right into the arms of a Cowboy defender. Game over. I jumped off the couch and screamed at the screen as Eli walked off the field, head down in that dejected pose of his when he throws an interception. "Jesus Christ, what's the matter with you?"

Immediately Kevin reminded me of our surroundings. "Dad, the funeral."

I noticed that the constant buzz from downstairs had suddenly stopped, now replaced with an eerie silence. To this day, I worry that I may have sent a fragile worshipper in the midst of a crisis of faith over the edge. Did I inadvertently send a message this person could easily have misinterpreted, confirming their doubts? It would be difficult, I must admit, to deny a booming voice from above intoning the very words that may have been central to one's spiritual struggle.

Oh dear, such are the concerns and predicaments of life six feet over.

# Jane's Underground Eulogy

All of us instinctively know that funerals are for the living. Far too often, we let the dead orchestrate the proceedings by abiding too strictly to what is written in the will, assuming this is what our loved one would have wanted. After all, it is the living who need the ritual that a funeral service is designed to provide. By celebrating the life of the deceased and grieving publicly, we are granted the opportunity to find some sort of closure. A well-crafted eulogy can be instrumental in helping people take comfort as they are reminded of the stories, experiences, and character of their departed love one.

When our older sister Jane died, the five remaining siblings were not given any substantial roles in the funeral. Jane was adamant that her nun friends would organize it. It would have been appropriate for one of us to eulogize our sister, but no one asked us, and none of us volunteered. You wouldn't expect this from a family of Irish-Catholic storytellers, but we were conflicted since Jane was not going to be an easy person to eulogize. Not only were our relationships with her generally complicated, but there was the matter of living up to the purpose of the eulogy which is simply to praise. No one felt up to the Herculean task of balancing this praise with some semblance of truth.

Just before my brother Dick got up at the end of the funeral and thanked the large group for coming, there was some muttering among the siblings that I should get up and say something, but it was too late, and I was too unprepared. We were disappointed that the eulogizers had sugarcoated Jane's life. When the service ended, we felt no sense of closure or proper grief. I was kicking myself for not taking on the role of family eulogizer as I had done previously at our brother Drew's funeral.

So, the next week, I set about writing Jane's underground eulogy that I then circulated to family members and selected others like a subversive newspaper in the old Soviet Union. My huge regret is that I never got to deliver it at her funeral...

The Eulogy

Jane Correa Maggin.  Those are three names we never heard together.
Jane never went for hyphens and after her divorce never returned to
Correa. It was always Jane Maggin.  Strange, don't you think, for a woman
who was somewhat of a player in the women's movement?  Jane, however, had no use for gaining equality with men.  She did her best to out-
fox, out-compete, and outright annihilate her unsuspecting counterparts.
When asked at women's forums what the secret was, her answer was
quite prosaic:  "Learn the accounting procedures.  Know how to crunch
the numbers."  In Jane's view, it wasn't about manipulation but rather
beating the "good old boys" at their own game.

Jane loved family, the idea of family, and the reality of the various
facets she experienced.  She was so proud that her daughter, Alice,
came out well: so highly-educated, so successful in her line of work
as a television producer, so considerate of others, especially the less
fortunate, and such a good mother.  But she was probably most relieved
that her daughter had somehow survived childhood on a steady diet of
Lucky Charms.

Remarkably, Alice became an excellent gourmet cook despite the
gastronomically-disadvantaged household in which she was raised.  Jane
would have been the first to admit that she wasn't much of a cook.  She
treated cooking as if it were an extracurricular activity, like Latin club, that
she chose not to participate in.  With Jane, it was all about ordering a
special cut of roast beef from her butcher at the Jefferson Market, not
what was supposed to happen next in the kitchen.

Jane had a special appreciation for Alice's husband, Wayne Nelson.
Of course, she loved the way Wayne treated Alice and her granddaughter,
Lila, but it probably had more to do with how Jane and her son-in-law
were the antithesis of each other.  The tall, quiet, reserved Texan and
the loud, boisterous, exuberant New Yorker brought together by life's

circumstances really did appreciate each other. Wayne has an uncanny knack for staying on the periphery, away from the noisy big-family fray. You'll never see anyone hover over the barbecue or endlessly landscape a postage-stamp-sized plot quite like Wayne does at the beach house. Eventually, you would seek out Wayne for some "quiet" conversation...

Jane absolutely adored her granddaughter, Lila. Lila is the spitting image of Alice at this age. It's scary when you compare the pictures; they might as well have been twins! And they would have been a pretty even match for precociousness when we remember back to little Alice. At three years old, after a morning of dazzling her pre-school classmates and teachers with her gifted intelligence, Lila would be off to her afternoon cooking class. One day, she reported back that she had made a very yummy couscous. Then it was back to her nanny to brush up on her Spanish...What's next from Lila, Alice? *Mommy, in case you're wondering, I'm meeting some friends for lunch. Can't miss the sale at Bloomingdales...* Sorry Alice, game, set and match to Lila! Jane, whenever feeling despondent, regretted that she wasn't going to see Lila grow up. Unfinished business, just part of the deal.

Jane's relationships with her siblings were a bit more complicated. The oldest of seven is not something you would ever volunteer for. Childhood, in her case, was cut short by the surrogate mother role, and there wasn't a lot of quality time with Mom and Dad as younger brothers and a sister seemed to appear overnight. Unbeknownst to some is just how competitive big families really are. The physical resemblances may be striking, but the behavior screams out rugged individualists. One of the important roles that siblings play in a big family is to never under any circumstances give credit to another brother or sister for any achievement in the outside world. I once made a game-winning basket in a middle school game. The discussion at the dinner table that night centered on the turnover when I dribbled the ball off my foot.

Jane craved recognition from the family and would often brag to us about some accomplishment. We would collectively cringe as she went on and on, and then we gave her the old "ho hum" as we did our best to change the subject. What Jane never understood was that her siblings were motivators par excellence and that we were actually doing her a service. Would there have been an Addie May Collins Anti-Poverty Agency? A Vice-Presidency at NYU? A "Hands Across America" campaign so well organized? A chapel at the Convent of the Sacred Heart so beautifully renovated? Hell no! Thanks to her six siblings maintaining a united front, Jane Correa had something to prove, and the world at large benefited!

Yes, Jane was different from the rest of us. In a family of runners, avid hikers, vegetarians, and general health freaks, Jane moved to the beat of the proverbial "different drummer." She was the progenitor of the power nap. Jane could fall asleep anywhere, any time, under any conditions. Yes, probably even on a bed of nails! As far as lifestyle choices go, it wasn't that she just smoked like a chimney; it was more like the eternal flame that never went out. She puffed heavily from the time she was a teenager and never once professed the slightest desire to quit. The only surprise was that she didn't get lung cancer. And Jane wasn't shy about drinking. She missed the cocktail hour about as often as a Trappist monk oversleeps early morning vespers... Nevertheless, Jane was a decent athlete. She once scored thirty-six points in a high school basketball game at Red Bank Catholic, and she loved tennis. Her game, however, was more grit than technique. For years, a doubles match was a Bay Head beach house ritual.

Jane was not raised in the city but became a New Yorker through and through. She left suburban Little Silver, New Jersey to make to her mark in the Big Apple as a young woman and immediately did so. Yet, it wasn't until she moved to the Village in the 70's that she really hit her stride. As a bigwig at NYU, she became a force in the neighborhood as well as a player in the transition and growth that the university was experiencing.  Jane lived in a beautiful apartment at 37 Washington Square West overlooking the park.  She generously opened her door to many of her twenty-something siblings mired in that "in between stage" who needed a place to crash. We all got to experience her famous "red couch" treatment.  Located in her paneled living room, this couch was the ultimate in sleeping comfort. I was there for a number of months teaching at NYU's American Language Institute.  I couldn't help noticing her long hours.  Jane would leave at 7:30 AM and often not return until 10:00 PM or later.  She was a workaholic, but also she did have a knack for incorporating her social life into her work life by going out to dinner virtually every night.  Alice as a young girl would often call Jane's office pleading that she come home at once...

Jane was way ahead of the curve when it came to child care.  She had a live-in student who took care of Alice and a devoted caretaker and maid, Luz, who just loved Jane and adored Alice.  It was Luz that Jane turned to in the last weeks of her life when she needed a reliable hospice nurse.  Luz came out of retirement to answer the call, working steadily into exhaustion to help and comfort her dear Mrs. Maggin.

When Alice and Jane's sister, Kate, were going through her possessions, stuffing garbage bags full of old clothes to give to Good Will, they discovered Jane's acceptance letter from Harvard Business School. Jane always told the story that Dad was against her going on the grounds that she was a woman.  She was never one to be shy about stretching the truth or adding a little hyperbole for flair and self-promotion, but we all knew the much more mundane real story. Like many parents with a brood of college-eligible offspring looming on the horizon, Dad had simply drawn the line at graduate school tuition.  And, as the fates would have it, in no way did Jane miss out on a successful career as a business woman.

Kate and Alice also happened upon a letter Jane wrote to Mom and Dad when she was sixteen describing how she was seriously thinking of becoming a nun and that she needed an immediate response from them.  We'll never know what advice Mr. and Mrs. Correa gave their eldest daughter, but the evidence of Jane's life would suggest that it went something like this: *No, Jane.  You are not to become a nun.  You will, however, spend the rest of your life surrounded by them.*

In the last month of her life, Jane was adamant about going down to her beach house in Bay Head over the Memorial Day weekend.  She was so happy to have Kate, her only sister, and an actual hospice nurse, in from New Mexico. Kate was truly instrumental in the way she lovingly helped Jane accept her impending death.

The trip from New York City was stressful, and it was clear that this would be her last time at the Jersey shore.  Her breast cancer had metastasized, and now the end was near.  As we were sitting on the beach for the final time, Jane asked me to guide her back to the house as she was once again feeling exhausted and needed to take a nap.

When we got to her bedroom, Jane collapsed on the bed and said, "Johnny, this is no way to live." And of course it wasn't as she suffered with constant stomach pains and vomiting.

"You know Jane," I said, realizing that I was now embarking on one of those summative big  picture conversations, "Life is a journey."

"I agree," Jane said softly.

"We're here to learn lessons," I continued.

"I've learned enough lessons.  I'm done," Jane responded, both defiantly and with resignation in her voice.

Jane then mentioned Kevin.  "Yeah, I guess he came out alright," I noted like most fathers would.

"He's such a gentleman," Jane said and began to cry...

I changed the subject.  "Do you remember the time when I was in fourth grade and you took me to a Red Bank Catholic football game? It was one of those beautiful early-October Saturday afternoons, the high blue sky bathed in golden autumnal light, and we were tooling around Red Bank in your friend's red convertible?

Her eyes were closing now. "Well Jane, thanks for being so generous." And I quietly left my sleeping sister in peace.

Ironically, it was not Jane's last trip to the beach. A week after her death, family members gathered on a jetty off the beach at Bay Head late one afternoon. We waited for the lifeguards to leave and then began to spread Jane's ashes into the Atlantic Ocean. Thankfully there was a south breeze behind us so that we didn't suffer the indignity of the ashes blowing back in our faces! The ocean on this particular day was especially big, wide, and expansive as the clear blue sky and endless sea merged at some faraway horizon.

The ashes formed a sandy colored cloud and then began to drift out to sea where they were cleansed and ultimately absorbed by the timeless lapping of the waves. So elemental, the physical material of the body returning to the source of its life---the mighty primordial ocean from whence it came. Just as soul, too, returns to its true ocean of love and mercy... Goodbye Jane, bon voyage.


July 10, 2008

# Dear Shoeless Joe

What's up with your museum in Charleston? The true believers were making some noise last week.  Seems they had asked the Major League Baseball Commissioner to rescind your lifetime suspension posthumously and reinstate you to the game you have always loved.  Commissioner Manfred issued his ruling last week with an emphatic "No!" which pretty much will keep your suspension in place throughout eternity. But be honest with me, Shoeless Joe, was this just a publicity stunt to beef up the declining attendance at your museum?  Or are you just stuck on this baseball immortality thing?

Now listen to me Joe, be a little reasonable here.  Could you let go a little?  How about we take stock and see if you can be a little less hell-bent on clearing your name, OK?  The direction of your ultimate journey is at stake here, so for God's sake, Shoeless Joe, please take in what I have to say.

Your status, Joe, as a baseball immortal and a folk hero of mythic proportions is and will always be intact and secure.  You were a giant of the game and true representative of our national pastime as the great pastoral game in the early part of the twentieth century.  Born in poverty in Pickens County, South Carolina, you remember working those twelve-hour shifts at the local textile mill in Brandon as a six-year-old sweeping cotton dust off the wooden floors, don't you? You just hated being called a "linthead," but you had no choice as dire as your family income needs were.

Working in the factory meant you never went to school, making you illiterate, which haunted you all your life, even as you became a star player.  The embarrassment always persisted as you did everything you could to mask your inability to read. The other players rode you so unmercilessly that you even quit a couple of times and returned to South

Carolina. Hard to believe that the greatest hitter ever got bullied as an adult as badly as any awkward elementary kid on the school playground.

Going out to dinner with the other ballplayers, you would pretend to read the menu and then order whatever you heard another player order. Nowadays, we've got plenty of non-English speakers playing at the Major League level with so many Hispanic ballplayers and even a few Japanese and Korean. I bet, knowing you, Shoeless Joe, you would have gone out of your way to help them feel comfortable and welcome as you empathized with their situation. Still, it's inspiring to see the adversity you overcame and your determination to be the best ballplayer there ever was.

Your escape and passion even as a little kid was baseball. I, too, used to eat, sleep, and breathe the game as well. Coming from a big family like you did, my four brothers and I played not only hardball but all the variations that involved a ball, bat, and glove: softball, stickball, shagging fly balls, running bases, and playing catch. I also was fortunate to play second base in Little League and then continue into Babe Ruth League.

One memory that I will always cherish, Joe, is something that we had in common as ballplayers. We both had our special bats. You had "Black Betsy," and I had "The Log." Now, Black Betsy was of mythic proportions. It was your one-and-only bat that you played with for twenty-four years. It was made out of hickory, and you would soak it in a barrel of oil between games. I know Roy Hobbs's bat, "Wonderboy," from the movie *The Natural* was cut from a lightning struck tree, but it had nothing on Black Betsy. The great hitter, Ted Williams, would visit the Louisville Slugger factory in Kentucky during the off season to pick out his bats. He always claimed that a bat only had so many hits in it before it should be discarded no matter its condition. Black Betsy defied that sort of reasoning and makes the bats of today with their pencil-thin handles that break so frequently look like toothpicks.

Now Joe, I had "The Log." It was a Nellie Fox signature bat. He was a line-drive hitter for the Chicago White Sox in the 50's and early 60's. Like Black Betsy, it was indestructible. The handle was so wide you could still hit a decent line drive even if you got jammed by a pitch. My greatest baseball achievement was the Babe-Ruth-League game in which I went five for five. The Log was magical that day. It seemed like I just stuck it out there and I was hitting line drives all over the place.

I never allowed my special bat to mix in with the other bats in fear it would be chipped or worse yet, lost. I took it home with me after every game and stored in a safe spot in my bedroom closet. I loved to pull it out and take a few practice swings after I woke up in the morning.

By the time I was fifteen, some of the physically mature pitchers could not only bring major heat, but some were throwing roundhouse curves as well. I never learned how to hit those. I kept bailing out. Wish you could have taught me, Joe. I was done, left with only my dreams of playing more organized ball.

Remember when you were thirteen and got called into the office at the mill? Probably thought you were going to be fired and then get a whupping from your father. The boss, much to your surprise, asked if you wanted to play for the Brandon Mill team. You were the youngest player ever to be on the team, and they paid you $2.50 to play once a week on Saturdays. I bet you couldn't believe you were getting paid to play baseball. Your hitting was so exceptional that you became a celebrity around town. They called your home runs "Saturday Specials" and your line drives "Blue Darters." Eager fans flocked to the games to see the kid who could hit like no one else, a true baseball phenom.

I still wonder Joe, talent's one thing , but with your brutal work schedule, how did you ever find enough time to hone your skills and play enough games to develop and improve? Ted Williams, who is in your class as one of the greatest hitters of all, and the last man to hit .400 (.406 in 1941) used to hit until his hands bled. I bet your five brothers took turns pitching to you whenever work was done, especially since you were the oldest and had the powers of "persuasion" on your side.   I had four brothers, and we played all sports until we were called in when it got dark. 'Course we only had school to occupy us, not a twelve-hour shift in a mill.

Before you knew it, you were off as a green-eyed country bumpkin to a tryout in 1908 for a minor league team, the Greenville Spinners.  You arrived at the ballpark carrying your special bat, "Black Betsy", and a few threadbare clothes stuffed into a cardboard suitcase.  Soon after you made the team, your new spikes were causing blisters so painful you went to bat in your socks and hit a triple.  Some fan yelled out "You shoeless son of a gun," and the name stuck immediately.  They started you out as a pitcher, but after you broke your catcher's arm with a sizzling fastball, just about everybody was afraid to bat against you.  Holy Jesus, you could pitch, too!  The manager was looking for a way to keep you in the lineup with your prodigious hitting, so moving you to the outfield was a no-brainer.  It worked out quite well, didn't it Joe, as you got to hit every day and were able to demonstrate your tremendous ability.

By 1911, you made it to the major leagues and hit .408 for the Cleveland Indians, a record for  rookies that still stands today as does your Major League record of twenty-six triples in 1912.  By comparison, the 2015 Major League leader hit only fifteen.  Ty Cobb said you were the best hitter he had ever seen, and Babe Ruth modeled his hitting technique after yours.  Previous to you, hitters slapped at the ball and didn't generate much power.  The Babe saw in your full-out, powerful swing the means by which he would eventually become one of the greatest home-run-hitters ever. When asked what is the secret to hitting a baseball, a player of your era, Hall of Famer Wee Willie Keeler, said "I hit 'em where they ain't."  You demonstrated this maxim, Joe, better than anyone  by your uncanny ability to hit line drives into the gaps in both left and right field.

Amazing, Joe, that you never won a batting title.  "I hit .408, .395, and .373, and I ain't won nothing yet."  Well, only because the Ty Cobb was a contemporary of yours.  Otherwise, you would have won a bunch of them.  It also blows my mind, Joe, that you averaged thirty outfield assists per season your first three years.  The league leader now throws out about fifteen.  You would have thought that no base-runner would have been crazy enough or stupid enough to  attempt to take an extra base on your cannon of an arm!  Is there anything you didn't master in this game?

Now Shoeless Joe, keep in mind that you have also been immortalized in the cinema.  I know, even up there, you've seen the movie *Field of Dreams* more than a few times. Aren't you flattered that the Iowa farmer that Kevin Costner plays hears a mysterious voice that instructs him to build a baseball diamond in a cornfield so you, Shoeless Joe Jackson, can play baseball again.  Must have felt good, Joe!   "If you build it, they will come...."

OK, so no doubt your baseball immortality is guaranteed. Now, the hard part is your banishment from the game, which means, as you well know, that you will never enter the Baseball Hall of Fame.  This is hard, Shoeless Joe, because it seems so unfair.  After meticulously looking at all the evidence, I seriously doubt that you were in on the fix.  After all, the grand jury acquitted you of any wrongdoing.  It was the uncompromising Commissioner Landis who wanted to make an example out of you by sanctimoniously playing the platitude cards of "the integrity of the game" and "restoring public confidence."  The  devastating lament of the disillusioned young fan that ran up to you after the hearing in which you were banished from baseball for life and said, "Say it ain't so, Joe, say it ain't so" surely didn't help your case in the court of public opinion.

Yet there is evidence that you refused the $5,000 bribe on two occasions and that you tried to tell the White Sox owner about the fix, but he refused to meet with you.  You were unable to afford legal counsel, so you were represented by the White Sox team attorney which was a clear conflict of interest. This deceitful lawyer, Alfred Austrian, was able to persuade you to sign a waiver of immunity from prosecution. Jesus, Shoeless Joe, once again done in by your illiteracy. Never thought about learning how to read during the off season?

And let's not forget that years later, the seven other players implemented in the Black Sox Scandal confirmed that you were never at any of their planning meetings to fix the World Series games. But to me, the clincher has to be your actual performance in the 1919 Fall Classic. You hit .375, made no errors, and threw a guy out at the plate. Hardly sounds like a ballplayer on the take, does it?

At least one consolation in all of this is that you weren't suspended for life early in your career. You were, after all, Joe, thirty-three years old when the banishment came down. No longer young for an athlete, and you did get to play Major League baseball for thirteen years. In your last year, 1920, before the scandal broke, you had another banner year, hitting .382 and showing no signs of slowing down. Who knows how much longer you could have continued at that level? Sad fact is we'll never know, Shoeless Joe.

But it's what you said in your interview with the Sporting News in 1942, long after your major league career so suddenly ended, that makes me feel that you're going to be alright Joe.

"Regardless of what anybody says, I didn't do nothing wrong. I was innocent of them charges. I gave baseball all I had. The Supreme Being is the only one I got to answer to. If I had been out there booting balls and looking foolish at bat against the Reds, then there might been some reason to believe I was in on it. I think my record in the 1919 World Series will stand up against any other man in that Series, or any other World Series in all history."

Precisely, Joe. And this, coupled with all your good work coaching and helping to develop young ballplayers in South Carolina after your banishment, demonstrates your good heart and lack of bitterness.  Yes, Mr. Shoeless Joe Jackson, you are more-than-ready to answer the call and now go wherever your Supreme Being decides to take you.  This chapter, this lifetime is now closed.  The Baseball Hall of Fame is small potatoes in comparison to the other worldly  "Hall of Fame" to which I believe you can freely aspire.

Thanks for listening, Shoeless Joe.

Best regards,

John, your fan for the ages

# The Bricklayer

Jack Miller died the other day. The last time I saw him he was propped up in a deck chair on his front porch, a shrunken skeleton, dressed in a bright yellow terry cloth robe and tattered black slippers.

"Those sons of bitches," he railed. "I felt alright until they made me go to the hospital. The god damn testing's killing me." Jack bit his lip and gazed off at the parched hills in the distance. He turned and nodded quietly. "Hell of a deal, eh?"

Jack was a union mason. He rose in his time from hod carrier to foreman. "I'm a bricklayer," he used to say, eschewing pretense. "I don't go for the fancy titles." Nor did he look blue collar. The somber brown eyes, groomed gray hair, and distinguished good looks could easily have passed for those of a retired business executive, that is, if he never took his hands out of his pockets. They were a battered testament to a life of labor: thick, gnarled fingers; palms laced with scraggly white scars; and skin, what was left of it, rough as sandpaper.

Jack took disability retirement in his early sixties. "I was around a lot of asbestos. They sprayed it on steel frames as a fire retardant and used it in floor tiles and pipe insulation. And nobody was taking precautions back then." Despite three palliative surgeries for his work-related lung cancer, Jack stood firm and upright when I first met him.

In 1983, I was renting a dilapidated cottage in the Bayview neighborhood of San Francisco about a mile from Candlestick Park. My elderly landlord, who had no patience for dealing with predatory real estate agents, offered to sell it to me for $35,000. By San Francisco standards, even back then, this was a steal!

I had just begun working on the place when Jack poked his head in the door one day. "So you're gonna fix up the old shack?" he asked, glad to see the neighborhood eyesore restored.

"Yeah, old lazy Louie," Jack sighed, looking around at the general state of disrepair. "Here's another place he let go. Never fixed anything if he could put a band-aid on it. Course I can't complain too much. He never gouged me on the rent although I've sure done my share of painting, plumbing, and general fixing up. Hell, I even put a patio in the back. Wouldn't you know, the roof's got a bad leak in it now, but I don't trust myself on a ladder no more. Them days are over."

However, his tinkering days were not. If it wasn't a toaster, he'd be taking apart his pickup. There was always a project and plenty of garage sales and flea markets to peruse for something Jack could put to good use. Admittedly, he was a sucker for bargains. "Just can't resist 'em..."

A few days later, Jack stopped in for another look. He watched me wielding the sledgehammer.

"You ever done this before?"

"No, I haven't."

Jack chuckled. "It's always a lot easier to knock 'em down than put 'em up..." He then took a closer look at the wall where I had ripped off some of the sheet-rock.

"It's all redwood. They sure don't make 'em like this anymore. How old's this place?"

"I'm not exactly sure. But it survived the 1906 earthquake."

"Is that right?" Jack said, eyes perking up. "Mind if I take a look in the basement?" he asked already half-way down the stairs.

Jack put on his reading glasses and examined the foundation. "Get a priest," he deadpanned. "See how the ceiling's sagging? If you don't do something about this real soon, the whole front of the house is gonna cave in."

Jack stepped back and took off his glasses.

"Now, the first thing you do is get some 4 by 4's and wedge 'em in there. That'll help prop up the ceiling. Clear out all this crumbling brick. Then you'll be ready to build on top of the original foundation. It's in pretty good shape. At least it ain't going nowhere."

Jack arrived early the next morning. "You got those 4 by 4's in place?" he asked gruffly. "Good. Now you got some support," he said, shaking one to see just how much. "OK, hold this," he commanded, pulling out a tape measure. He scribbled down some numbers and drew a diagram. "I'll go home and figure out what you're gonna need."

Jack reappeared after lunch. "I got it all worked out. Now get these materials," he said, handing me a list.

The materials arrived the next day. Piled on the sidewalk were 196 cinderblocks, 6 bags of cement, 3 bags of lime, and a cubic yard of sand.

"Uh, uh...Jack."

"Relax. I'll guide you through it. But can't help much with this," he said, trying to flex his hand. "I fell off a ladder painting the house a while back. Severed a nerve. Can't handle the trowel. Lost my grip."

The next day, we began work in earnest. The remaining foundation was uneven, so we filled it in with leftover bricks and pieces of cinderblock until we had a level three-foot base. Now we were ready to build to the basement ceiling in new cinderblock. I began the first row or course as they call it in the trade. Jack put the level on it.

"Rip it out," he barked. "It ain't true. In this business, son, it's either perfect, or you hang it up." I tried again, but it still wasn't right.

Jack grabbed the trowel. "You're gonna be my hod carrier," he exclaimed in exasperation. Using his left hand he went to work, and I began mixing mortar.

"Too dry. Too wet. Too thick. Too thin. I like my mud to go on like soft butter," he yelled, whipping his apprentice into shape.

Jack wasn't strong enough to lift the cinderblocks, so we worked out a system. He mudded up the ends of the blocks and I lifted them into place. Then, Jack made the final adjustments, tapping each block into place and scraping off any excess mortar.

The neighbors and passers-by were drawn to the exposed foundation. Jack accepted these frequent interruptions to catch his breath. "Couldn't do it without my able assistant," he'd say with a wink.

By noon time, Jack was finished for the day. His wife, Betty called him for lunch on the stroke of twelve. "Coming babe," he would shout cheerfully up the street.

Late one morning, Jack began to wheeze fitfully. Leaning against the half-completed wall he gasped between breaths, "I'm gonna take an early lunch."

Half an hour later, Jack popped his head in the door. "Let's go," he said, impatiently picking up his trowel.

We completed the project on a warm Indian summer day in November. The sky was high and clear. There was a sense of urgency knowing the colder weather would soon make its inevitable return. We'd been at it over a week and were looking forward to finishing. I went right to work mixing up a fresh batch of mortar. Either it was the right consistency, or Jack was tired of complaining.

As the sun climbed higher in the sky, our final rows kept pace. Jack was now smiling as he stopped to clean his trowel. Instead of starting the last row from one end and working clear across to the other, he began to work from the ends toward the center.

I picked up the final cinderblock. Jack applied the mortar, and I lifted it into place. It fit like the last piece of a jigsaw puzzle. Jack tapped the block. He scraped off the excess mortar. He stepped back. He scrutinized the completed foundation with the demanding eye of a foreman inspecting someone else's work. He nodded his head. "That's my last piece of work."

Little did I know when we began our renovation project together that it would become such a profound undertaking. Jack modeled for me, his fledgling student, what mastery entails. We were also left with a renewed foundation that embodied a strong and solid mix of the old and the new. And I got to witness a consummate craftsman signing off on his last little gem while acknowledging his impending death.

I tried, but Jack refused any money. "How about a bottle of whiskey?" That night we drank a toast.

"To the hod carrier."

"To the bricklayer."

# Acknowledgments

Special thanks to two exceptional writing professors at the Santa Fe Community College.

Miriam Sagan is a very accomplished poet and fiction writer as well as a gifted teacher. She provided the deadlines I needed to develop my writing discipline as well as pinpointed feedback and encouragement.

Daniel Kilpatrick worked with me to revise and edit the stories. He had an extraordinary knack for making suggestions to help strengthen the stories and get them to work better as narratives.

A slew of family and extended family members both Correas and McCarthys as well as friends gave valuable feedback. Bill, the storyteller, made helpful contributions. And thank you Kevin and Sarah for your enthusiastic responses and encouragement, and Mary, Kate, and Lisa for your edits and thorough proofreading.

# About The Author

John Correa is a retired school teacher and administrator who lives in Santa Fe, New Mexico. His big family upbringing taught him that in order to hold court he better get to the point quickly or risk being heckled off stage. Embellishment, exaggeration, and stretching the truth a bit all make for good storytelling. Once the audience is laughing , you've got 'em.

And no, he never thought living above a funeral home was weird. Isn't death part of life?

Comments welcome at: johnnykcap@yahoo.com

Made in the USA
Charleston, SC
14 January 2017